United States

HARCOURT BRACE SOCIAL STUDIES

FLORIDA Daily Reading Support
for Social Studies

Harcourt
SCHOOL PUBLISHERS

Orlando   Austin   New York   San Diego   Toronto   London

Visit *The Learning Site!*
www.harcourtschool.com

Grateful acknowledgment is made to Japanese American National Museum for permission to reprint from "Letter to Clara Breed" dated April 13, 1942, by Tetsuzo Hirasaki. Gift of Elizabeth Y. Yamada, Japanese American National Museum (93.75.31G).

Printed in the United States of America

ISBN 0-15-341051-5

1 2 3 4 5 6 7 8 9 10   082   14 13 12 11 10 09 08 07 06 05

Contents

Name _____ Date _____

Compare and Contrast

Directions Read the paragraph below. Then use the information, and what you know about Florida, to complete the graphic organizer. Compare and contrast what Florida was like long ago with what Florida is like today.

During the Ice Age lower water levels in the ocean made Florida's land area about twice as large as it is today. Florida's climate was much cooler and drier. Early Floridians usually camped near springs or shallow lakes, where they hunted animals such as giant land tortoises, giant sloths, mastodons, and mammoths. People hunted these animals for meat, and they used the skins and bones to make clothing, tools, and weapons.

REMEMBER:

• **When you compare information, you are showing how things are alike, or similar. Words such as *like*, *both*, *also*, and *similarly* are used in comparisons.**

• **When you contrast information, you are identifying how things are different. Words such as *instead*, *but*, and *however* are used in contrasts.**

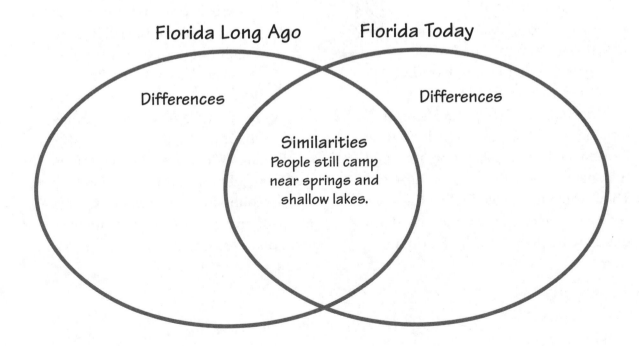

Florida Long Ago   Florida Today

Differences   Differences

Similarities
People still camp
near springs and
shallow lakes.

LA.A.2.2.7(5.1) extends the expectations of the fourth grade with increasingly complex reading selections, assignments and tasks (for example, textual organization, comparison and contrast).
LA.E.2.2.4(5.2) identifies the major information in a nonfiction text.

Lesson 1: The Search for Early Peoples

Building Text Comprehension
Compare and Contrast

Directions Read the passage below. Then use the information from the passage to complete the graphic organizer on the next page. Compare and contrast scientists' views with those of the Seminoles on how all living things, including early people, came to the Americas.

Florida was a different place long ago. Water was trapped in the glaciers, and at several different times the level of the oceans dropped and a large "bridge" of dry land appeared between the continents of Asia and North America.

Some scientists believe that between 12,000 and 40,000 years ago, hunting groups from Asia began crossing the land bridge into North America. By 12,000 years ago they had made their way to what is now Florida.

Others believe that the first Americans could have come here earlier by other ways. For example, in northern Florida, archaeologists found a mastodon tusk near the Aucilla (aw•SIH•luh) River. They were very excited when they found cut marks on one end of the tusk that were made by the tools of early Floridians.

Using scientific methods, the archaeologists learned that the tusk was 12,200 years old. Because of discoveries like this one, some scientists think that the first Americans may have come to the Americas earlier by boat.

Native Americans, however, believe that the first Americans did not come from Asia or by boat but that they were always here. Native Americans tell stories about the origins, or beginnings, of their people.

The Seminoles of Florida believe that Native Americans have always lived in the Americas. They also tell a story about the Creator, the Grandfather of all things. He made all living things. He put them all into a large shell that he placed in the mountains. When the shell cracked, all the living things came out and found their places on Earth.

(continued)

LA.A.2.2.7(5.1) extends the expectations of the fourth grade with increasingly complex reading selections, assignments and tasks (for example, textual organization, comparison and contrast).
LA.E.2.2.4(5.2) identifies the major information in a nonfiction text.

Name _____ Date _____

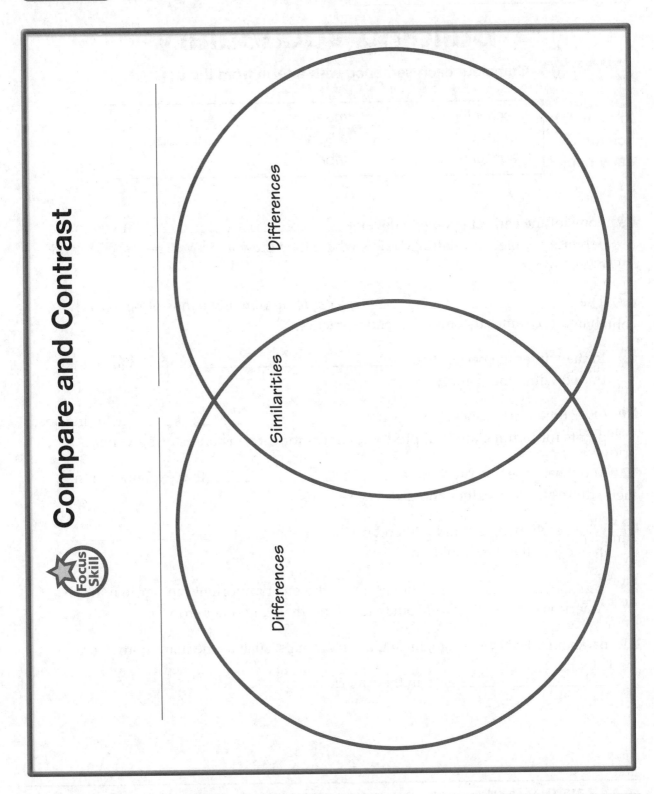

Compare and Contrast

Focus Skill

Differences

Similarities

Differences

LA.A.2.2.7(5.1) extends expectations of the fourth grade with increasingly complex reading selections, assignments and tasks (for example, textual organization, comparison and contrast).
LA.E.1.2.3(5.3) knows the similarities and differences of events presented within and across fifth grade or higher level selections.

Reading Support for Social Studies

Lesson 2: Ancient Indians

Building Vocabulary

Directions Complete each sentence with a term from the box.

technology	maize	surplus
extinct	religion	specialize
agriculture	tribe	

1 Some of the earliest people to develop _____ lived in the Tehuacán Valley in Central Mexico, where they grew avocados, beans, corn, and other crops.

2 The _____ was made up of many bands of people who shared the same customs, ideas, and practices.

3 In the winter the people had a _____ of food, which they traded with other bands.

4 Over time, early tribes developed new _____, including spear points for hunting and leakproof containers for carrying and storing water.

5 Many early people practiced a _____ that explained things in nature such as weather and growing seasons.

6 When early people could get food easily, some began to _____ in one job that they could do well.

7 _____, or corn, was the most important food grown in the Americas because it gave people more food than any other crop.

8 By about 10,000 years ago, most giant mammals, such as the mammoth, were

_____ in the Americas.

© Harcourt

LA.A.1.2.3(5.1) uses a variety of strategies to determine meaning and increase vocabulary (for example, homonyms, homophones, prefixes, suffixes, word-origins, multiple meanings, antonyms, synonyms, word relationships).
LA.A.2.2.1(5.1) extends previously learned knowledge and skills of the fourth grade level with increasingly complex reading texts and assignments and tasks (for example, explicit and implicit ideas).

Lesson 3: Early Civilizations

Building Fluency

Directions Part A. Practice reading the terms aloud.

Vocabulary		Additional Terms	
civilization	pueblo	basalt	Cahokia
temple	adobe	Mound Builders	Pueblo Bonito
pyramid	mesa	obsidian	Chaco Canyon
cultural diffusion	drought		
earthwork	kiva		

Directions Part B. First, practice reading aloud the phrases. Then, practice reading aloud the sentences.

1 An Olmec temple / was sometimes built / on top of a pyramid.

2 Basalt was a type of rock / that the Olmecs used / to carve giant stone heads.

3 The spread / of the Olmec culture / to other places / is known as cultural diffusion.

4 The ancient civilizations / known as Mound Builders / built earthworks.

5 The Hopewell civilization / made spear points and knives / from obsidian.

6 Archaeologists estimate / that as many as 40,000 Mississippians / lived in the city of Cahokia.

7 A pueblo home was made / from adobe / and usually sat / on top of a mesa.

8 Pueblo Bonito / was built / beneath Chaco Canyon / in New Mexico.

9 Since drought was common, / the Anasazi dug holes and ditches / to store water.

10 An Anasazi religious service / was held / in a kiva.

Directions Part C. Turn to page 62 in your Student Edition. Read aloud the first 2 paragraphs three times. Try to improve your reading each time. Record your best time on the lines below.

Number of words	99
My best time	___
Words per minute	___

LA.A.1.2.4(5.1) uses a variety of strategies to monitor reading in fifth-grade or higher level texts (for example, adjusting reading rate according to purpose and text difficulty, rereading, self-correcting, summarizing, checking other sources, class and group discussions, trying an alternate word).

FCAT

FCAT Test Prep

Directions Read the passage "Mound Builders of Florida" before answering Numbers 1 through 8.

Mound Builders of Florida

About 12,000 years ago, the region that is now Florida was cool and dry. Most water was found in deep, open springs. When animals gathered at the springs to drink and graze, they became targets for early hunters.

By about 5,000 years ago, the climate had become more like it is today. Early people traveled shorter distances to find water and to hunt. Some began to settle in one place and grow crops. They fished in the rivers and the ocean for food.

Early people threw food leftovers, seafood shells, and other garbage into *middens*, or trash piles. Today archaeologists learn about the diet, tools, and weapons of early people by studying these middens.

Over thousands of years, some middens grew into wide, high mounds. About 2,000 years ago, Native Americans began burying their dead in some of the mounds. They built temples and houses at the top of other mounds.

Today the remains of ancient mounds can be found around Florida. Several are protected as state parks, including Turtle Mound at Cape Canaveral National Seashore, Crystal River Archaeological State Park, and Lake Jackson Mounds State Archaeological Site.

Turtle Mound is located on Florida's east coast. It began as a shell heap about 1,200 years ago. Today it rises more than 30 feet high. Archaeologists have found oyster shells, animal bones, and pieces of ancient pottery in Turtle Mound.

Directly west of Turtle Mound, on the Gulf Coast, is the Crystal River Mound site. The area has six mounds. Archaeologists found graves in two of the mounds. Several of the mounds are flat on top and, at one time, had stairways going up the sides. Archaeologists believe that these mounds were used as stages for religious ceremonies.

The Lake Jackson Mounds lie far to the northwest, near Tallahassee. They were built about 1,000 years ago. By the 1500s the area had six mounds, a village, and a plaza. Native Americans gathered at the Lake Jackson Mounds to celebrate, trade, and bury their dead.

© Harcourt

Go On ▶

Name _____ Date _____

Directions Now answer Numbers 1 through 8. Base your answers on the passage "Mound Builders of Florida."

1 What is the main idea of the fourth paragraph?

Ⓐ Middens became large enough to be used in other ways.

Ⓑ Middens were used continuously for thousands of years.

Ⓒ Native Americans built temples at the top of mounds.

Ⓓ Native Americans buried their dead in mounds.

2 Which of the following artifacts will archaeologists NOT find in a midden?

Ⓕ shells

Ⓖ animal bones

Ⓗ pottery

Ⓘ adobe bricks

3 Why do archaeologists study mounds?

Ⓐ so they can build their own mounds

Ⓑ to learn about the ancient cultures of the southeastern United States

Ⓒ because they are the only archaeological sites in Florida

Ⓓ to learn about the diets of prehistoric animals

4 Which of the following statements is NOT true?

Ⓕ The remains of ancient mounds can be found all over Florida today.

Ⓖ Turtle Mound rises more than 30 feet high.

Ⓗ All mounds are peaked on top.

Ⓘ The Lake Jackson site has six mounds.

5 In this passage, the word *mound* means

Ⓐ a deep, open water hole.

Ⓑ a hill that people built up over thousands of years.

Ⓒ an ancient pile of trash.

Ⓓ a stage used for religious purposes.

6 The Crystal River Archaeological State Park is located

Ⓕ north of Turtle Mound.

Ⓖ on the Atlantic Ocean.

Ⓗ 10 miles north of the Lake Jackson Mounds.

Ⓘ on the Gulf Coast.

© Harcourt

Go On ▶

FCAT

7 List and explain the various ways that Native Americans used mounds.

READ THINK EXPLAIN

_____

_____

_____

_____

_____

_____

_____

8 Explain how we know about the ways Native Americans used mounds.

READ THINK EXPLAIN

_____

_____

_____

_____

_____

_____

_____

STOP

© Harcourt

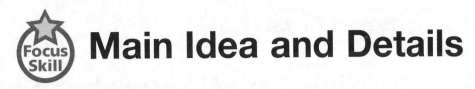

Main Idea and Details

Directions Read the paragraph below. Then use the information to complete the graphic organizer. Identify the details about the Native Americans of Florida.

More than 350,000 Native Americans lived in Florida when the Spanish arrived in the early 1500s. The Apalachees lived in the northwestern corner of Florida, the Timucuas in the northern and central regions, and the Calusas in the south. Although each group spoke a different language, they shared similar ways of life. They farmed the same crops, lived in huts made of woven sticks and mud, and followed religions based on nature. The Spanish brought diseases that killed many Apalachee, Timucuan, and Calusa Indians. Others died in wars or were enslaved by the Spanish. By the middle of the 1700s, all of Florida's original Native American groups had died out.

REMEMBER:
- **The main idea of a paragraph or lesson is what it is mostly about. The main idea may be stated in a sentence, or it may only be suggested.**
- **Details give more information about the main idea.**

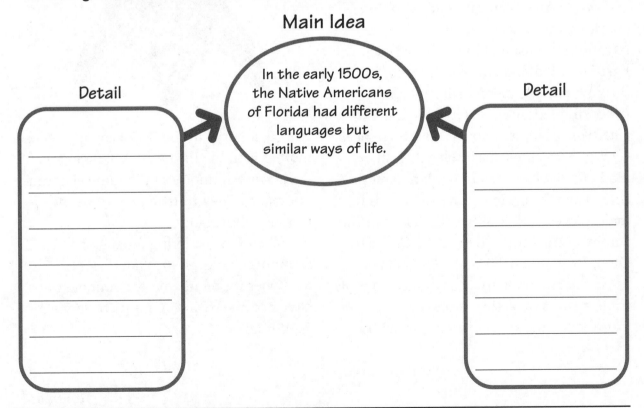

Main Idea

In the early 1500s, the Native Americans of Florida had different languages but similar ways of life.

Detail

Detail

LA.A.2.2.1(5.1) extends previously learned knowledge and skills of the fourth grade level with increasingly complex reading texts and assignments and tasks (for example, explicit and implicit ideas).
LA.E.2.2.4(5.2) identifies the major information in a nonfiction text.

© Harcourt

Lesson 1: Northwest Coast

 Building Text Comprehension
Main Idea and Details

Directions Read the passage below. Then use the information from the passage to complete the graphic organizer on the next page. Identify the main idea and details about Native American clans in North America.

The word *clan* describes family groups within a tribe or community. Clans are found in communities around the world. For example, some families in Scotland and Ireland are divided into clans. Many clans follow ancient traditions. One Scottish tradition is for clan members to wear skirts known as kilts, which are woven with the clan's special colors and patterns.

Native American tribes are also divided into clans. Both the Chinooks of the Northwest Coast and the Iroquois of the Eastern Woodlands trace their ancestors through clans. Other North American tribes divided into clans include the Cherokees, Hopis, Ojibwas, and Shawnees.

The Seminole tribe of Florida is also made up of clans. Seminole clan names come from things in nature, such as animals, places, and weather. The clans of the Seminole tribe include the Bear, Bird, Deer, Otter, Panther, Snake, and Wind clans.

In the Seminole tribe, as in the Chinook tribe, clan membership is passed on through the mother. For example, a boy

whose father is in the Bear clan and whose mother is in the Bird clan will be in the Bird clan. Seminoles of the same clan cannot marry. They must marry someone from another clan.

When the last living female of a Seminole clan dies, the clan dies, too. Over the years, many Seminole clans have become extinct. One such clan is the Turtle clan.

(continued)

© Harcourt

LA.A.2.2.1(5.1) extends previously learned knowledge and skills of the fourth grade level with increasingly complex reading texts and assignments and tasks (for example, explicit and implicit ideas).
LA.E.2.2.4(5.2) identifies the major information in a nonfiction text.

Name _____ Date _____

Directions Complete the graphic organizer.

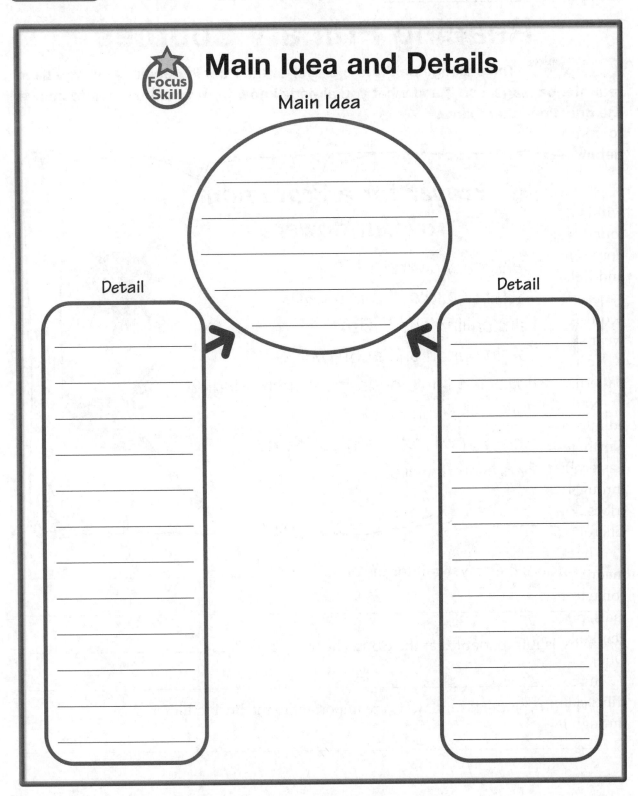

Main Idea and Details

Main Idea

Detail

Detail

LA.A.2.2.1(5.1) extends previously learned knowledge and skills of the fourth grade level with increasingly complex reading texts and assignments and tasks (for example, explicit and implicit ideas).
LA.E.2.2.4(5.2) identifies the major information in a nonfiction text.

Name _____ Date _____

Reading Primary Sources

Directions The passage below is a prayer of the Pueblo people. After you have read the passage, use it and what you already know from your textbook to answer the questions that follow.

Prayer for a Profusion of Sunflowers

Send sunflowers!
With my turkey-bone whistle
I am calling the birds
To sing upon the sunflowers.
For when the clouds hear them singing,
They will come quickly,
And rain will fall upon our fields.
Send sunflowers!

1 Why does the prayer call for the birds? _____

_____

2 Why is it important that the clouds hear the birds? _____

_____

3 Why do you think sunflowers are important to the Pueblo Indians?

_____

_____

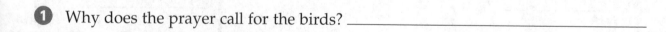

LA.E.1.2.1(5.3) reads a variety of literary and informational texts (for example, fiction, drama, poetry, myths, fantasies, historical fiction, biographies, autobiographies, textbooks, manuals, magazines).

© Harcourt

Lesson 3: Great Plains

Building Fluency

Directions **Part A. Practice reading the terms aloud.**

Vocabulary		Additional Terms	
lodge	tepee	buffalo	jerky
sod	travois	Mandans	Kiowas

Directions **Part B. First, practice reading aloud the phrases. Then, practice reading aloud the sentences.**

1. Earth lodges / were covered / with sod.

2. There were anywhere / from 12 to 100 / earth lodges / in a single village, / and each lodge was home / to several families.

3. Twice a year, / the Mandans walked / for several days / to participate / in a great hunt.

4. Buffalo was often dried / to make jerky, / so that the meat / could be kept longer.

5. Although they claimed certain areas, / such as western Montana, / the Kiowas were nomads.

6. A travois / was made from the wooden poles / in a tepee / and used to carry goods.

Directions **Part C. Turn to page 81 in your Student Edition. Read aloud the first 2 paragraphs three times. Try to improve your reading each time. Record your best time on the lines below.**

Number of words	100
My best time	____
Words per minute	____

LA.A.1.2.4(5.1) uses a variety of strategies to monitor reading in fifth-grade or higher level texts (for example, adjusting reading rate according to purpose and text difficulty, rereading, self-correcting, summarizing, checking other sources, class and group discussions, trying an alternate word).

Lesson 4: Eastern Woodlands

Reading Biographies

Directions Read the passage about Betty Mae Tiger Jumper.

Betty Mae Tiger Jumper
Character Trait: Citizenship

Betty Mae Tiger Jumper was born on April 27, 1923, in a Seminole camp near Indiantown, Florida. She grew up in Dania, in Broward County.

At night Tiger Jumper listened as older members of the tribe told stories passed down from their ancestors. "The stories taught you how to live," she says. She would later write down these stories to preserve them for future generations. Before she could do that, she had to learn how to read and write.

At that time Seminole children were not allowed to attend public schools in Florida. Tiger Jumper decided to attend a boarding school for Native Americans. She became the first Seminole to learn to read and write English and the first to graduate from high school.

Tiger Jumper continued her education and became a nurse. She traveled to Seminole towns to care for members of her tribe. She also wrote books and worked as the editor of a newspaper now called the *Seminole Tribune*.

In 1967 Tiger Jumper became the first female chair, or chief, of the Seminole tribe. When Tiger Jumper became chief, the tribe had just $35 in savings. Thanks to her leadership, the tribe had $500,000 when she left office in 1972. She also brought together several tribes to form an organization that runs health and educational programs for its members.

"I had three goals in my life," Tiger Jumper says. "To finish school, to take nurse's training and come back and work among my people, and to write three books." She has met those goals and many more. A Florida legend, Tiger Jumper was inducted into the Florida Women's Hall of Fame in 1994.

(continued)

© Harcourt

LA.E.1.2.1(5.3) reads a variety of literary and informational texts (for example, fiction, drama, poetry, myths, fantasies, historical fiction, biographies, autobiographies, textbooks, manuals, magazines).
LA.E.2.2.4(5.2) identifies the major information in a nonfiction text.

Name _____ Date _____

Directions After you have read the biography on page 14, write details about Betty Mae Tiger Jumper's life in the boxes below.

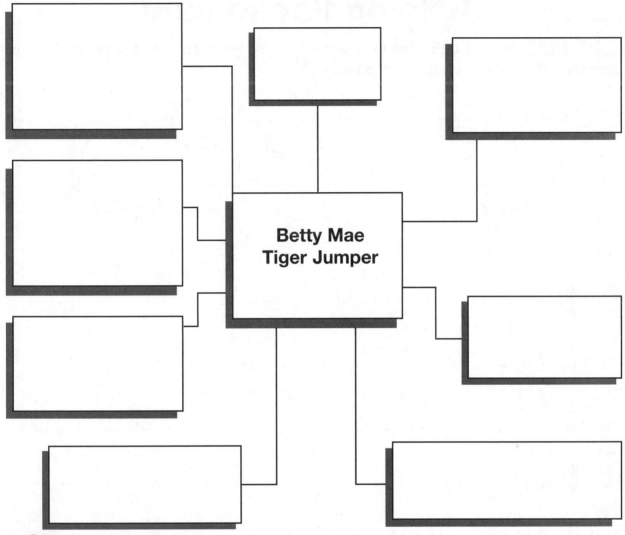

Betty Mae
Tiger Jumper

Use the details above to write a sentence about how Betty Mae Tiger Jumper demonstrated **citizenship**.

_____

_____

_____

_____

LA.E.1.2.1(5.3) reads a variety of literary and informational texts (for example, fiction, drama, poetry, myths, fantasies, historical fiction, biographies, autobiographies, textbooks, manuals, magazines).
LA.E.1.2.2(5.3) makes inferences and draws conclusions regarding story elements of a fifth grade or higher level text (for example, the traits, actions, and motives of characters; plot development; setting).

© Harcourt

Lesson 5: Middle America

Building Vocabulary

Directions Write a definition in your own words for each vocabulary term. Then complete the activity on the next page.

1 city-state _____

_____

2 class _____

_____

3 noble _____

_____

4 slavery _____

_____

5 empire _____

_____

6 emperor _____

_____

7 tribute _____

_____

(continued)

LA.A.1.2.3(5.1) uses a variety of strategies to determine meaning and increase vocabulary (for example, homonyms, homophones, prefixes, suffixes, word-origins, multiple meanings, antonyms, synonyms, word relationships).
LA.A.2.2.1(5.1) extends previously learned knowledge and skills of the fourth grade level with increasingly complex reading texts and assignments and tasks (for example, explicit and implicit ideas).

Reading Support for Social Studies   **16**   Use with Chapter 2, Lesson 5.

© Harcourt

Name _____ Date _____

Directions Use the vocabulary terms from page 16 to complete the word box below. Replace the underlined words in each sentence with the correct vocabulary term. Write the vocabulary term in the box next to the corresponding sentence.

Sentence	Vocabulary Term
The Aztec <u>ruler</u> led a civilization of more than 5 million people.	
Most Mayan nobles believed in the practice of <u>holding people against their will and making them carry out orders.</u>	
The Olmecs, the Maya, and other Indian nations were divided into <u>groups of people treated with different amounts of respect in their society.</u>	
In the Mayan culture, <u>people from important families</u> ruled along with the priests.	
The Aztecs conquered 200,000 square miles (518,000 sq km) in Middle America to form <u>an area of many peoples and places ruled by an emperor.</u>	
The Aztec ruler demanded <u>payments</u> from the conquered people.	
The Mayan civilization was made up of <u>cities with their own rulers and governments.</u>	

LA.A.1.2.3(5.1) uses a variety of strategies to determine meaning and increase vocabulary (for example, homonyms, homophones, prefixes, suffixes, word-origins, multiple meanings, antonyms, synonyms, word relationships).
LA.A.2.2.1(5.1) extends previously learned knowledge and skills of the fourth grade level with increasingly complex reading texts and assignments and tasks (for example, explicit and implicit ideas).

© Harcourt

FCAT Test Prep

Directions Read the passage "The Timucuas" before answering Numbers 1 through 7.

The Timucuas

The Timucuas lived in northern Florida, between the Atlantic coast and the Aucilla (aw•SIH•luh) River. Their lands reached north into present-day Georgia and south almost to where the city of Orlando is now located.

Much of what is known about the Timucuas and other groups of Native Floridians comes from the writings and drawings of early European explorers. One of them was Jacques Le Moyne (ZHAHK luh•MWAHN), a French mapmaker and artist, who visited Florida in 1564. Le Moyne's drawings and the descriptions written by other explorers have given historians a picture of the lives of the Timucuas and other Native Floridians.

The Timucuas used wood from the surrounding forests to carve tools and dugouts. They also built their houses from wood. They used wooden poles and posts to make a round frame and then covered it with palm fronds.

About 150 Timucuan villages were spread across northern Florida. Each village had a council house, a building in which leaders met to make decisions for the village. People also gathered there for special events.

In addition to wood, the forests provided food for the Timucuas. They gathered wild fruits and nuts and hunted the deer, bears, turkeys, and other animals that lived there.

The waterways in northern Florida were another important resource for the Timucuas. They could travel on them in dugouts to visit other villages and to trade goods. The waterways also provided the Timucuas with fish and shellfish.

To help catch the fish, the Timucuas used weirs (WIRZ). A weir is a fence built across a river to trap fish. The Timucuas made their weirs from sticks and stretched them across streams where they flowed into estuaries, or mouths of rivers. Fish swam over the top of a weir as they entered the stream with the rising tide. As the tide fell, the fish were trapped behind the weir, and the Timucuas could easily spear or net them.

© Harcourt

Go On ▶

Directions Now answer Numbers 1 through 7. Base your answers on the passage "The Timucuas."

1 Which statement is the BEST summary for this passage?

Ⓐ The Timucuas were good traders.

Ⓑ Jacques Le Moyne was an important explorer.

Ⓒ The Timucuas used the natural resources around them to survive.

Ⓓ Timucuan villages were spread across the state.

2 How have historians learned about the lives of the Timucuas?

Ⓕ from books left by the Timucuas

Ⓖ by asking present-day Timucuas about their ancestors

Ⓗ by studying the cave paintings left by the Timucuas

Ⓘ from the writings and drawings of European explorers

3 The Timucuas caught fish easily because

Ⓐ they built weirs to trap the fish.

Ⓑ they wove large and sturdy nets.

Ⓒ the waterways in northern Florida were not very deep.

Ⓓ European explorers taught them how to fish.

4 How did the Timucuas build their houses?

Ⓕ by making mounds of earth

Ⓖ by stacking stones and sticking them together with mud

Ⓗ by using poles and posts to make a round frame and covering it with palm fronds

Ⓘ by baking bricks in the sun and using clay to make them stick together

5 The author wants the reader to think that the Timucuas

Ⓐ knew little about hunting.

Ⓑ were creative in adapting to their environment.

Ⓒ were fierce and warlike.

Ⓓ did not travel outside their villages.

6 Which of the following is NOT true?

Ⓕ The Timucuas gathered wild fruits and nuts in the forests.

Ⓖ The Timucuas got all of their food through farming.

Ⓗ The waterways allowed the Timucuas to trade with other villages.

Ⓘ The Timucuas used weirs to catch fish.

Go On ▶

Name _____ Date _____

7 The Timucuas ate a variety of foods. Write a paragraph explaining what those foods were and how the Timucuas collected them.

READ
THINK
EXPLAIN

_____

_____

_____

_____

_____

_____

_____

_____

_____

_____

_____

_____

_____

_____

_____

_____

_____

_____

STOP

Name _____ Date _____

Sequence

Directions Read the paragraph below. Then use the information to complete the graphic organizer. Identify the order of the events.

In 1450 Johannes Gutenberg invented a new way to print books. After his invention came into use, books could be printed more easily and for less money. One popular book of the time was written by Marco Polo. In his book he describes Asia. After reading the book, many Europeans became interested in the wealth and goods described in it. Before long, European merchants began traveling to Asia.

REMEMBER:
- **Sequence is the order in which one event comes after another.**

- **Words like** *first*, *then*, *next*, *before*, *after*, **and** *later* **indicate sequence.**

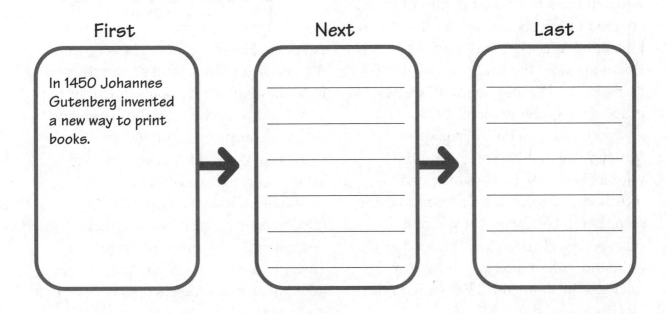

First

In 1450 Johannes Gutenberg invented a new way to print books.

Next

Last

© Harcourt

LA.A.2.2.1(5.1) extends previously learned knowledge and skills of the fourth grade level with increasingly complex reading texts and assignments and tasks (for example, explicit and implicit ideas).
LA.A.2.2.5(5.1) reads and organizes information from multiple sources for a variety of purposes (for example, supporting opinions, predictions, and conclusions; writing a research report; conducting interviews; taking a test; performing tasks).
LA.E.2.2.4(5.2) identifies the major information in a nonfiction text.

Lesson 1: A Legendary Land

Building Text Comprehension
Sequence

Directions Read the passage below. Then use the information from the passage to complete the graphic organizer on the next page. Identify the sequence of events.

Leif Ericsson (LAYV AIR•ik•suhn) was a Norse explorer who lived about 980 to 1025 A.D. He became the leader of the first established settlement in Greenland. Many now believe that Ericsson led the first European journey to North America.

How did Ericsson reach North America? First, in about 1000 A.D., Ericsson hired a crew to sail west to find new land. He had heard stories of a land covered in forests and small hills. When he landed in present-day Canada, Ericsson called the land *Vinland*, or "vine land," because he found many grapevines growing there.

Next, Ericsson built a village in Vinland. He and his crew spent the winter there. After that winter, they returned to Greenland. Ericsson told the colonists in Greenland stories of his discoveries. He described Vinland as a rich land, full of forests and meadows.

Then, in about 1025, Ericsson died. His discovery did not lead to any permanent settlements in North

Leif Ericsson

America. However, many believe that the people of Greenland often returned to Vinland after Ericsson's death. In the 14th and 15th centuries, the Greenland colony disappeared. But Ericsson's stories survived. He became the Viking spirit of exploration.

Finally, about the year 1200, the *Greenlanders' Saga* was written, describing Ericsson's voyage to Vinland. The *Greenlanders' Saga* has survived to this day. Archaeologists now believe that it is a fairly accurate account of the voyages of the Vikings.

© Harcourt

(continued)

LA.A.2.2.1(5.1) extends previously learned knowledge and skills of the fourth grade level with increasingly complex reading texts and assignments and tasks (for example, explicit and implicit ideas).
LA.E.2.2.4(5.2) identifies the major information in a nonfiction text.

Name _____ Date _____

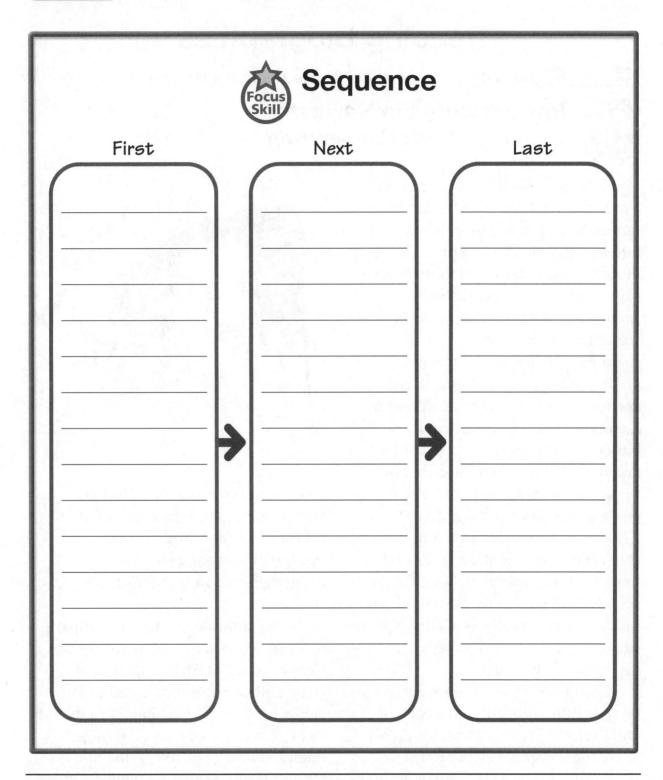

Sequence

First → Next → Last

LA.A.2.2.1(5.1) extends previously learned knowledge and skills of the fourth grade level with increasingly complex reading texts and assignments and tasks (for example, explicit and implicit ideas).
LA.A.2.2.5(5.1) reads and organizes information from multiple sources for a variety of purposes (for example, supporting opinions, predictions, and conclusions; writing a research report; conducting interviews; taking a test; performing tasks).
LA.E.2.2.4(5.2) identifies the major information in a nonfiction text.

Lesson 2: Background to European Exploration

Reading Biographies

Directions Read the passage about Prince Henry the Navigator.

Prince Henry the Navigator
Character Trait: Cooperation

In the early 1400s most ships sailed along merchant routes in the Mediterranean Sea. Only a few ventured west into the Atlantic Ocean. Prince Henry of Portugal was determined to send more ships into the Atlantic. He began to sponsor, or pay for, voyages along the western coast of Africa.

In 1419 Henry moved to Sagres on the southern tip of Portugal. He surrounded himself with people who knew about sailing, including shipbuilders, astronomers, cartographers, and instrument makers. Together they came up with ways to make sailing on the ocean safer and faster.

One of Henry's achievements was a ship called a *caravel*. Most ships of that time were large, heavy galleys. Galleys sat low in the water, so they could not sail near rocky coastlines. Caravels were smaller and faster than galleys, and they sat higher in the water.

When Henry was 34 years old, his brother Pedro brought him a copy of *The Travels of Marco Polo*. Marco Polo's adventures inspired Henry to keep sponsoring voyages. He wanted to find

an all-water route to India. In 1434 Henry's persistence paid off when his captain sailed around Cape Bojador. It was one of the most dangerous sections of the African coastline.

By the time Henry died, his ships had reached as far as the mouth of the Gambia River in Africa. Because of Henry, other Europeans dared to sail along the African coastline. Even though Henry never took an ocean voyage, English speakers gave him the title "Prince Henry the Navigator."

(continued)

© Harcourt

LA.E.1.2.1(5.3) reads a variety of literary and informational texts (for example, fiction, drama, poetry, myths, fantasies, historical fiction, biographies, autobiographies, textbooks, manuals, magazines).
LA.E.2.2.4(5.2) identifies the major information in a nonfiction text.

Name _____ Date _____

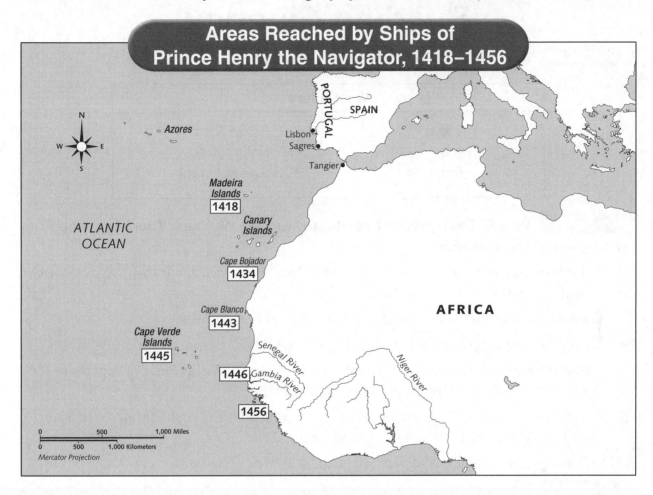

Areas Reached by Ships of Prince Henry the Navigator, 1418–1456

1. What was the name of the city Henry moved to in 1419? Circle it on the map.

_____

2. What was a caravel? Why could it be called one of Henry's achievements?

_____

3. Draw a star on the map, near Cape Bojador. Why was it important to Henry?

_____

How did Prince Henry the Navigator demonstrate **cooperation**?

_____

LA.E.1.2.1(5.3) reads a variety of literary and informational texts (for example, fiction, drama, poetry, myths, fantasies, historical fiction, biographies, autobiographies, textbooks, manuals, magazines).
LA.E.1.2.2(5.3) makes inferences and draws conclusions regarding story elements of a fifth grade or higher level text (for example, the traits, actions, and motives of characters; plot development; setting).

© Harcourt

Lesson 3: *I, Columbus: My Journal 1492–1493*

Building Fluency

Directions **Part A. Practice reading the terms aloud.**

Vocabulary	
Indies	*Santa María*
Niña	unfurled
Pinta	San Salvador

Directions **Part B. First, practice reading aloud the phrases. Then, practice reading aloud the sentences.**

1 Columbus thought / that by sailing west, / he could reach the Indies / quicker than by sailing east.

2 The captain / of the *Santa María* / was Christopher Columbus.

3 The *Pinta*, / one of Columbus's ships, / spotted land / before any / of the others.

4 Two brothers experienced the journey / to the west, / Martin Pinzon, captain of the *Pinta*, / and Vincente Pinzon, / captain of the *Niña*.

5 When Columbus landed / on the island, / he unfurled the royal banner / of Spain / and claimed the land / for the king and queen.

6 Columbus named the island San Salvador, / to honor the Lord.

Directions **Part C. Turn to page 120 in your Student Edition. Read aloud the first 2 paragraphs three times. Try to improve your reading each time. Record your best time on the lines below.**

Number of words	**105**
My best time	_____
Words per minute	_____

LA.A.1.2.4(5.1) uses a variety of strategies to monitor reading in fifth-grade or higher level texts (for example, adjusting reading rate according to purpose and text difficulty, rereading, self-correcting, summarizing, checking other sources, class and group discussions, trying an alternate word).

Lesson 4: Early Voyages of Exploration

Building Vocabulary

Directions Each of the words below relates to early voyages of exploration to the Americas. Write each word from the Word Box next to its definition.

conclusion	expedition
isthmus	scurvy

1 a decision or idea reached by thoughtful study _____

2 a sickness caused by not getting enough vitamin C, which is found in fresh fruits and vegetables _____

3 a journey made for a special reason _____

4 a narrow strip of land that connects two larger land areas _____

Directions Answer the following questions.

5 Why do you think explorers, such as Ferdinand Magellan, led **expeditions**?

_____

_____

6 What are some of the **conclusions** Amerigo Vespucci formed on his voyage to the Americas? _____

_____

7 Where did a group of explorers discover an **isthmus**? _____

8 Why did some of the sailors on Magellan's ships develop **scurvy**?

_____

_____

LA.A.1.2.3(5.1) uses a variety of strategies to determine meaning and increase vocabulary (for example, homonyms, homophones, prefixes, suffixes, word-origins, multiple meanings, antonyms, synonyms, word relationships).
LA.A.2.2.1(5.1) extends previously learned knowledge and skills of the fourth grade level with increasingly complex reading texts and assignments and tasks (for example, explicit and implicit ideas).

FCAT Test Prep

Directions Read the passage "Legends of the Fountain of Youth" before answering Numbers 1 through 8.

Legends of the Fountain of Youth

Legends are stories handed down over time. In the 1500s one legend said that there was a special spring whose waters could make old people young again. Native Americans believed that this Fountain of Youth was on the island of Bimini (BIH•muh•nee), thought to be near the present-day Bahamas. A map published in 1511 showed the island located north of Cuba. The legend also said that Bimini had gold and other riches. No wonder Spanish explorer Juan Ponce de León (PAHN•say day lay•OHN) was interested in finding this island!

Ponce de León had sailed on Christopher Columbus's second voyage in 1493. Later, Ponce de León had helped take Puerto Rico from the Native Americans living there and had been made Puerto Rico's governor. He may have heard the Fountain of Youth legend from the Native Americans. Part of the story Ponce de León may have heard was about Arawaks who had traveled north from Cuba to present-day southern Florida. None of the Arawaks had returned to Cuba, so Ponce de León probably thought they had found what they were looking for.

Since this was not a new legend, it is also possible that Ponce de León had heard a similar legend from the time of Alexander the Great of Greece. Alexander was said to have looked for these waters in eastern Asia. The Polynesians had a legend, too, and they had been known to search in what is now Hawaii. Even an Italian geographer and historian had heard about the so-called Fountain of Youth. He wrote, "Among the islands of the north side of Hispaniola (ees•pah•NYOH•lah) . . . is a continual spring of running water, of such marvelous virtue that the water thereof being drunk, perhaps with some diet, maketh [makes] old men young again."

In 1513 Ponce de León left Puerto Rico with three ships. He planned to search for Bimini, its miraculous fountain, and its many riches. What he found instead was present-day Florida. He claimed the land for Spain and named it *La Florida*, which is Spanish for "flowery." Ponce de León did not find the legendary Fountain of Youth. As far as historians know, no one ever has.

Go On ▶

© Harcourt

Directions Now answer Numbers 1 through 8. Base your answers on the passage "Legends of the Fountain of Youth."

1 What is a legend?
  Ⓐ a true story
  Ⓑ a story handed down over time
  Ⓒ a fantasy
  Ⓓ a nonfiction account of an event

2 Where did Native Americans believe the Fountain of Youth was located?
  Ⓕ eastern Asia
  Ⓖ Hawaii
  Ⓗ Florida
  Ⓘ the island of Bimini

3 Which event occurred LAST?
  Ⓐ The Arawaks went in search of the Fountain of Youth.
  Ⓑ Ponce de León claimed *La Florida* for Spain.
  Ⓒ Ponce de León sailed with Christopher Columbus.
  Ⓓ Ponce de León became governor of Puerto Rico.

4 In addition to a miraculous fountain, Ponce de León hoped to find
  Ⓕ gold and other riches.
  Ⓖ the mainland of North America.
  Ⓗ the missing Arawaks.
  Ⓘ a water route that cut through North America to Asia.

5 Which statement is FALSE?
  Ⓐ Alexander the Great, Ponce de León, and the Arawaks may have searched for a special spring.
  Ⓑ Ponce de León found the legendary Fountain of Youth on the Gulf coast of Florida.
  Ⓒ A map published in 1511 showed that the island with a special spring was north of Cuba.
  Ⓓ Ponce de León named the land he found *La Florida*.

6 Which statement BEST describes the main idea of the passage?
  Ⓕ Ponce de León was the only person to search for a Fountain of Youth.
  Ⓖ None of those who went in search of the Fountain of Youth ever returned.
  Ⓗ There are many legends about a spring with water that can make old people young again.
  Ⓘ Native Americans were the only people who believed the legend about a special spring.

Go On ▶

© Harcourt

FCAT

7

READ
THINK
EXPLAIN

In the passage, several similar legends are mentioned. Tell how the legends are similar and and how they are different. Use details and information from the passage to support your answer.

_____
_____
_____
_____
_____
_____
_____

8

READ
THINK
EXPLAIN

Ponce de León went to search for the island of Bimini. Use details and information from the passage to tell what he found.

_____
_____
_____
_____
_____
_____
_____
_____

© Harcourt

Name _____ Date _____

 **Categorize**

Focus Skill

Directions Read the paragraph below. Then use the information to complete the graphic organizer.

Over time, many groups came to Florida. In the 1500s missionaries were sent to Florida by Spain to convert Native Floridians to Christianity. They were also sent to show the Native Floridians how the Spanish lived. This meant that the missionaries had to teach the Native Floridians the Spanish language, Spanish habits, and the Spanish style of dress. Two important missions in Florida were the Nombre de Dios (NOHM•bray day DEE•ohs) near St. Augustine and the Mission San Luis near present-day Tallahassee. Spanish soldiers also came to Florida. They came to the St. Johns River area and to St. Augustine to protect the missionaries and defend Spain's claim to Florida. Colonists came to Florida as well. They settled near the St. Johns River and in St. Augustine. Some colonists came to seek their fortunes; others came seeking religious freedom.

REMEMBER:

• **To categorize is to group information, or to sort information by category.**

• **People, places, and events can be placed in categories to make it easier to find facts.**

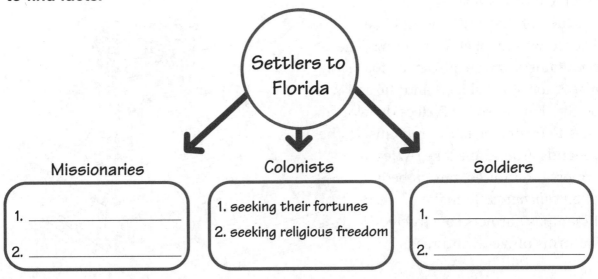

Settlers to Florida

Missionaries
1. _____
2. _____

Colonists
1. seeking their fortunes
2. seeking religious freedom

Soldiers
1. _____
2. _____

LA.A.2.2.1(5.1) extends previously learned knowledge and skills of the fourth grade level with increasingly complex reading texts and assignments and tasks (for example, explicit and implicit ideas).
LA.A.2.2.5(5.1) reads and organizes information from multiple sources for a variety of purposes (for example, supporting opinions, predictions, and conclusions; writing a research report; conducting interviews; taking a test; performing tasks).
LA.E.2.2.4(5.2) identifies the major information in a nonfiction text.

Name _____ Date _____

Lesson 1: Conquest of the Aztecs and Incas

⭐ Focus Skill Building Text Comprehension
Categorize

Directions Read the passage below. Then use the information from the passage to complete the graphic organizer on the next page. Categorize the city life, agriculture, and trade of the Aztec Empire.

The Aztecs built their capital city, Tenochtitlán, in a high mountain valley in what is today central Mexico. Tenochtitlán stretched over two islands in the middle of Lake Texcoco. By the 1500s it took up more than 5 square miles (13 sq km) and had more than 140,000 residents. The people of Tenochtitlán had specialized jobs. There were merchants, priests, politicians, and craftworkers. Outside Tenochtitlán, farmers raised corn, beans, squash, chili peppers, tomatoes, and other crops to feed the city's people.

Much of the land around Lake Texcoco was too wet for farming. The mountainsides were also poor for farming because they sloped and the soil was too dry. However, the Aztecs developed ways to overcome both problems. In the wetlands around the lake, Aztec farmers built raised garden beds called *chinampas*. To make chinampas, farmers constructed platforms of wood and reeds

above the water. On top of the platforms, they piled rich soil for planting. On the mountainsides, farmers carved terraces, or level steps of land. In addition, they built irrigation systems to water the crops.

The Aztecs traded for goods that they could not produce in their valley. Merchants led trading caravans south to the Gulf coast. There they exchanged salt, gold, and other goods for cotton, tobacco, honey, jewels, fine clothing, and cacao beans to make into chocolate.

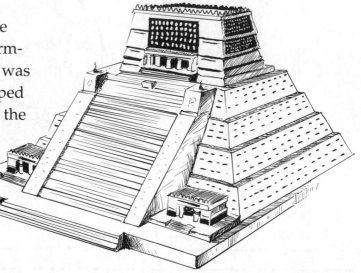

(continued)

LA.A.2.2.1(5.1) extends previously learned knowledge and skills of the fourth grade level with increasingly complex reading texts and assignments and tasks (for example, explicit and implicit ideas).
LA.E.2.2.4(5.2) identifies the major information in a nonfiction text.

Name _____ Date _____

Directions Complete the graphic organizer.

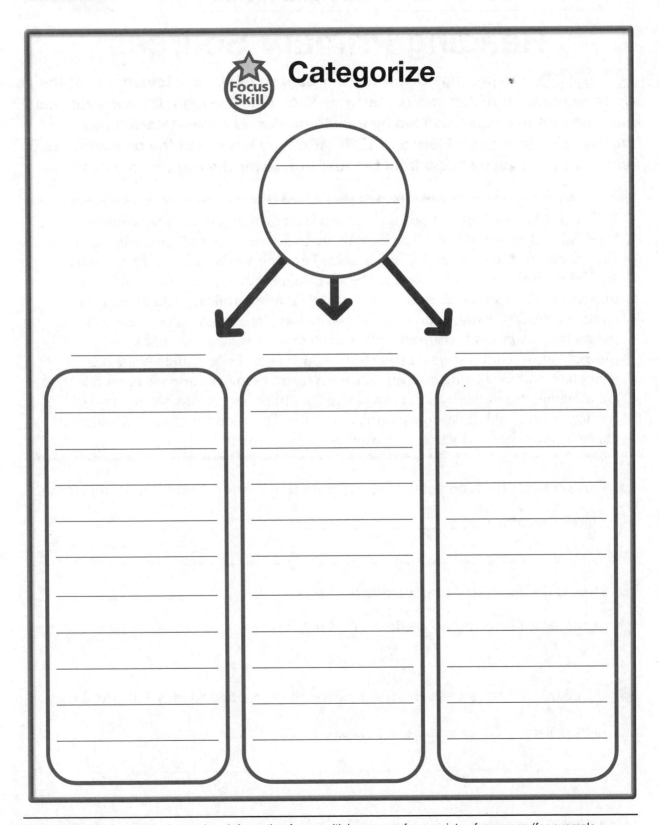

Categorize

LA.A.2.2.5(5.1) reads and organizes information from multiple sources for a variety of purposes (for example, supporting opinions, predictions, and conclusions; writing a research report; conducting interviews; taking a test; performing tasks).

Name _____ Date _____

Reading Primary Sources

Directions The passage below is from Cabeza de Vaca's *Adventures in the Unknown Interior of America.* **Cabeza de Vaca (kah•BAY•sah day VAH•kah) was a member of the expedition led by Pánfilo de Narváez (PAHN•fee•loh day nar•VAH•ays) to explore Florida in 1528. After you have read the passage, use it and what you already know from the text to answer the questions that follow.**

THE TERRAIN we had suffered through since first landing in Florida is mostly level, the soil sandy and stiff. Throughout are immense trees and open woods. . . . Everywhere are lakes, large and small, some hard to cross because of their depth and/or profusion of fallen trees. . . . The lakes in the Apalachen country are far larger than any we had seen earlier. This province has many cornfields, and houses are scattered over the countryside as at Gelves. We saw three kinds of deer; rabbits and jackrabbits; bears and lions [panthers]; and other wild animals, including one [the opossum] which carries its young in a pouch on its belly until they are big enough to find food by themselves; but, even then, if someone approaches while they are foraging, the mother will not run before the little ones get into her pouch. The country is very cold. It has fine pastures for cattle. The wide variety of birds in abundance includes geese, ducks . . . and numerous other fowl.

1 Do you think the members of the expedition in Florida found it to be a pleasant place? Explain. _____

_____

2 How did Cabeza de Vaca describe the lakes? _____

3 What resources did the expedition find in Florida? _____

_____

4 If Cabeza de Vaca and the rest of the expedition needed food, what could they have done? _____

_____

LA.E.1.2.1(5.3) reads a variety of informational texts (for example, fiction, drama, poetry, myths, fantasies, historical fiction, biographies, autobiographies, textbooks, manuals, magazines).
LA.E.2.2.4(5.2) identifies the major information in a nonfiction text.

Reading Support for Social Studies   34   Use with Chapter 4, Lesson 2.

© Harcourt

Lesson 3: New People in the Americas

Reading Biographies

Directions Read the passage about Tisquantum, also called Squanto.
Then use the information to answer the questions below.

Tisquantum (Squanto)
Character Trait: Cooperation

Tisquantum, known to the English as Squanto, was born in about 1585. He was a Native American of the Wampanoag (wam•puh•NOH•ag) tribe. When he was young, Squanto had been kidnapped and spent time as a slave in Spain. He escaped from Spain and fled to England. There, Squanto lived with Sir Ferdinando Gorges, who owned the Plymouth Company and used Squanto as a guide and interpreter.

After a time, Squanto returned to what is now Massachusetts. In 1621 he helped the Pilgrims by teaching them how to fish and plant crops. He also acted as interpreter for the Pilgrims and the Wampanoags in negotiating a peace treaty, the Treaty of Plymouth.

Squanto remained in the Plymouth Colony. He was a friend to Governor William Bradford. Squanto died in 1622. Governor Bradford wrote of his death, "In this place Squanto fell sick of an Indian fever . . . and within a few days died there; desiring the Governor to pray for him that he might go to the Englishman's God in Heaven; and bequeathed sundry [left various] of his things to sundry of his English friends as remembrances of his love; of whom they had great loss."

1 How did Squanto help the Plymouth colonists?

_____

2 How did Squanto feel about the English people he had lived with? How did they feel about him? How do you know?

_____

3 How is Squanto an example of the character trait **cooperation**?

_____

LA.E.1.2.1(5.3) reads a variety of informational texts (for example, fiction, drama, poetry, myths, fantasies, historical fiction, biographies, autobiographies, textbooks, manuals, magazines).
LA.E.1.2.2(5.3) makes inferences and draws conclusions regarding story elements of a fifth grade or higher level text (for example, the traits, actions, and motives of characters; plot development; setting).

Lesson 4: Encounters with the French and Dutch

Building Vocabulary

Directions Read each sentence. Then, on the line, write the term from the box that has the same meaning as the underlined words.

Northwest Passage	trade network	agent

1 Many early groups, including explorers, settlers, and Native Americans, used <u>a system of trading</u> to exchange goods that they produced for goods that they

could not produce. _____

2 The <u>person who does business for other people</u> exchanged goods for beaver furs with settlers on the frontier. He then traded the furs at the trading post for food, kettles, and tools. Finally, he returned to the frontier with a new load of

goods. _____

3 In the 1500s several European explorers spent their lives searching for a <u>water route that cut through North America to Asia.</u> _____

Directions Write two sentences about the French in North America using the terms in the box.

_____

_____

_____

_____

_____

LA.A.1.2.3(5.1) uses a variety of strategies to determine meaning and increase vocabulary (for example, homonyms, homophones, prefixes, suffixes, word-origins, multiple meanings, antonyms, synonyms, word relationships).
LA.A.2.2.1(5.1) extends previously learned knowledge and skills of the fourth grade level with increasingly complex reading texts and assignments and tasks (for example, explicit and implicit ideas).

Lesson 5: The English in the Americas

Building Fluency

Directions **Part A. Practice reading the terms aloud.**

Vocabulary		Additional Terms	
armada	compact	Roanoke	peninsula
profit	Mayflower Compact	Chesapeake	Tisquantum
pilgrim	interpreter		

Directions **Part B. First, practice reading aloud the phrases. Then, practice reading aloud the sentences.**

1 The island on which / Sir Walter Raleigh's colonists landed / was known as Roanoke / to the Hatteras Indians.

2 England defeated Spain's armada / in the late 1500s.

3 The Virginia Company of London / sailed into the Chesapeake Bay / in 1607.

4 The Virginia Company of London / wanted / to make a profit.

5 The English colonists / landed on a peninsula.

6 Pilgrims travel / to a place / for a religious reason.

7 The men aboard the *Mayflower* / signed a compact, / or an agreement.

8 The Mayflower Compact / is the first example / of self-rule / by colonists / in the Americas.

9 Tisquantum acted as an interpreter / for the Pilgrims.

Directions **Part C. Turn to page 151 in your Student Edition. Read aloud the first 2 paragraphs three times. Try to improve your reading each time. Record your best time on the lines below.**

Number of words	**93**
My best time	_____
Words per minute	_____

LA.A.1.2.4(5.1) uses a variety of strategies to monitor reading in fifth-grade or higher level texts (for example, adjusting reading rate according to purpose and text difficulty, rereading, self-correcting, summarizing, checking other sources, class and group discussions, trying an alternate word).

FCAT Test Prep

Directions Read the passage "The End of the Pequots" before answering Numbers 1 through 7.

The End of the Pequots

Native American tribes living in parts of New England during the 1600s did not want the colonists to take over their lands. Some of the colonists tried to live in peace with them. Other colonists thought they had a right to the land. Many colonists tried to change the way the Native Americans lived.

The Pequots (PEE•kwahts) were a powerful tribe. They lived along the Thames River in southeastern Connecticut. For some time the Pequots and the colonists living in the Massachusetts Bay Colony had disagreed over property, hunting, destruction of crops by settlers' livestock, dishonest trading, and other things. Although the Pequots needed to trade with the colonists, they were upset about losing the land they had lived on for years. In 1631 disagreements among tribe members caused some members to break away and form another tribe. Then in 1633 and 1634, many Pequots died from smallpox, causing the tribe to lose about half of its people.

After suffering tremendous losses and believing that they were being robbed of all that was important to them, the Pequots killed John Oldham, a dishonest trader. The colonists became angry, and the governor, John Endecott, organized a group of soldiers to punish the Pequots. The soldiers killed a small

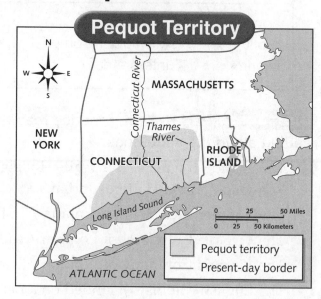

Pequot Territory

Legend: ▢ Pequot territory — Present-day border

number of Pequots living on Block Island. The remaining Pequots tried to get neighboring tribes to help them, but because the Pequots had fought in many wars with neighboring groups, none of the tribes would join them in the fight.

In May 1637 the soldiers attacked a main Pequot village, which was near what is today New Haven, Connecticut. More than 500 men, women, and children were killed, and the Pequot village was destroyed. Some Pequots were able to escape, but they were later captured and made to work as slaves for the colonists or were sold in the West Indies as slaves. Others were killed. Even the Pequot leader, Sassacus, was captured and later killed. Very few Pequots survived the war with the colonists. Those who did joined other tribes.

Go On ▶

© Harcourt

Directions Now answer Numbers 1 through 7. Base your answers on the passage "The End of the Pequots."

1 Which statement is the BEST summary for this passage?

Ⓐ Many Pequots were forced to work as slaves.

Ⓑ Native Americans did not want colonists on their land.

Ⓒ The Pequots started a war with the colonists by killing John Oldham.

Ⓓ Once a powerful tribe, the Pequots were eventually destroyed after attacks by the colonists.

2 Many colonists in New England

Ⓕ paid for their land.

Ⓖ avoided the Native Americans.

Ⓗ tried to change the way Native Americans lived.

Ⓘ wanted to live like the Native Americans.

3 In 1631 the Pequots lost some members because of

Ⓐ a smallpox epidemic.

Ⓑ disagreements among tribe members.

Ⓒ a battle with colonial soldiers.

Ⓓ disagreements over property.

4 Which of the following events happened FIRST?

Ⓕ Some Pequots died from smallpox.

Ⓖ John Oldham, a dishonest trader, was killed.

Ⓗ The Pequot leader, Sassacus, was captured and killed.

Ⓘ More than 500 Pequots were killed by soldiers.

5 The Pequots were unable to get neighboring tribes to help them fight the colonists because

Ⓐ the other tribes were afraid of the Pequots.

Ⓑ the Pequots were dishonest traders.

Ⓒ the Pequots had been warlike.

Ⓓ the other tribes were disagreeing among themselves.

6 All the following reasons contributed to the end of the Pequots EXCEPT

Ⓕ disagreements among tribe members.

Ⓖ their refusal to hunt.

Ⓗ an outbreak of smallpox.

Ⓘ attacks by soldiers on Pequot villages.

Go On ▶

FCAT

7 The colonists living in New England changed the lives of the Pequots. Explain how and why the colonists changed the lives of these Native Americans. Use details and examples from the passage in your explanation.

READ
THINK
EXPLAIN

_____

_____

_____

_____

_____

_____

_____

_____

_____

_____

_____

_____

_____

_____

_____

_____

© Harcourt

STOP

Summarize

Directions Read the paragraph below. Then use the information to complete the graphic organizer. Summarize facts about the Puritans.

Puritans were members of the Church of England, but they did not agree with many of its practices. Because of this, they came to North America to follow their religious beliefs in a "purer" way. They settled in the Massachusetts Bay area. One group of Puritans settled in Salem, and another group settled on the coast north of Plymouth. As other Puritan settlements were established, Salem and Plymouth served as models for Christian living.

REMEMBER:
- **When you summarize, you tell a shortened version of what you have just read.**

Facts

1. Puritans came to North America to follow their religious beliefs in a "purer" way.
2. They settled in the Massachusetts Bay area. One group settled in Salem, and another settled north of Plymouth.
3. Salem and Plymouth served as models for Christian living.

Summary

_____
_____
_____
_____
_____
_____

© Harcourt

LA.A.2.2.5(5.1) reads and organizes information from multiple sources for a variety of purposes (for example, supporting opinions, predictions, and conclusions; writing a research report; conducting interviews; taking a test; performing tasks).
LA.E.2.2.4(5.2) identifies the major information in a nonfiction text.

Name _____ Date _____

Building Text Comprehension
Summarize

Directions Read the passage below. Then use the information from the passage to complete the graphic organizer on the next page.

Missions in New Spain were built in the borderlands of the present-day states of Georgia, Florida, Texas, New Mexico, Arizona, and California. These missions were built because the Spanish king wanted to convert Native Americans to the Catholic faith. Some were also built to protect Spain's claims in New Spain. Farm buildings and churches were part of all missions. Many missions were built near Native American villages. Native Americans also often settled around them.

Some Native Americans raised food for the missions, such as corn, beans, and squash. In turn, missionaries taught Native Americans to use farm tools to

grow other crops, such as sugarcane, onions, and grapes. Native Americans learned a new way of worshipping as well. Some became Catholics; others kept the religion of their ancestors. However, some Native Americans were treated poorly and were forced to work on mission farms. In those places, they rebelled by destroying the missions.

Haciendas (ah•see•EN•dahs), large estates, were built in the borderlands of northern Mexico and in what would become Texas and California. Many crops, including wheat and sugar, were grown on haciendas. Cattle, sheep, and hogs were also raised there.

Many Native American workers were employed by ranchers, but they were paid very low wages—barely enough to live on. This meant that they often owed the ranchers money, so they had to remain on the haciendas.

Ranchers were self-sufficient—they grew or made everything they needed. As a result, communities grew far from the large cities of New Spain.

(continued)

LA.A.1.2.4(5.1) uses a variety of strategies to monitor reading in fifth-grade or higher level texts (for example, adjusting reading rate according to purpose and text difficulty, rereading, self-correcting, summarizing, checking other sources, class and group discussions, trying an alternate word).
LA.A.2.2.1(5.1) extends previously learned knowledge and skills of the fourth grade level with increasingly complex reading texts and assignments and tasks (for example, explicit and implicit ideas).
LA.E.2.2.4(5.2) identifies the major information in a nonfiction text.

© Harcourt

Name _____ Date _____

Directions Complete the graphic organizer.

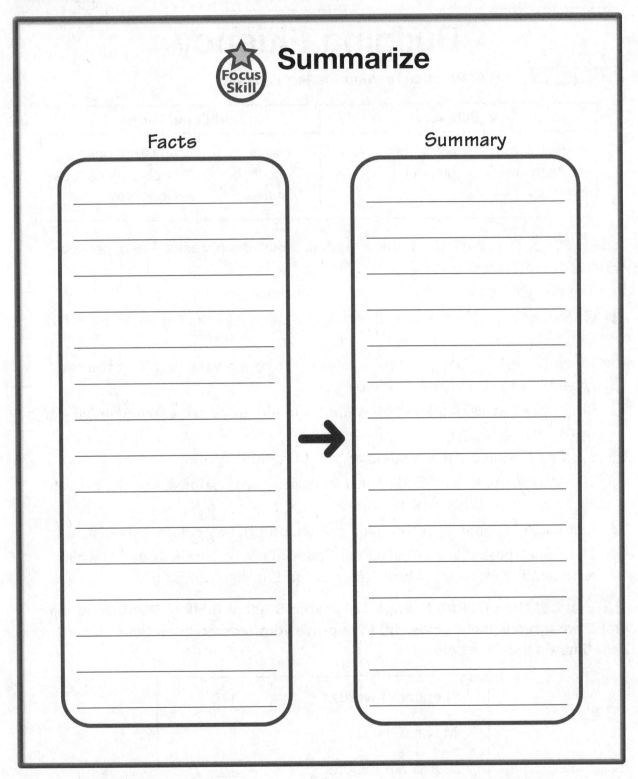

Focus Skill

Summarize

Facts

Summary

LA.A.1.2.4(5.1) uses a variety of strategies to monitor reading in fifth-grade or higher level texts (for example, adjusting reading rate according to purpose and text difficulty, rereading, self-correcting, summarizing, checking other sources, class and group discussions, trying an alternate word).
LA.E.2.2.4(5.2) identifies the major information in a nonfiction text.

© Harcourt

Lesson 2: The Growth of New France

Building Fluency

Directions Part A. Practice reading the terms aloud.

Vocabulary		Additional Terms	
royal colony	proprietary colony	fur trade	governor-general
portage	proprietor	Quebec	birch-bark canoes
tributary		Montreal	Code Noir

Directions Part B. First, practice reading aloud the phrases. Then, practice reading aloud the sentences.

1 The French / grew wealthy / from the fur trade.

2 Quebec and Montreal / were the only two cities / in New France / from 1608 to 1763.

3 When Louis XIV / declared New France / to be a royal colony, / governor-generals helped / to govern the people.

4 Birch-bark canoes, / made by the American Indians, / were light enough / to be carried on land.

5 The French called / this method of transportation / portage.

6 The Mississippi River / and all its tributaries / was claimed / for France / by Sir La Salle / and his expedition.

7 John Law / became the proprietor / of the proprietary colony, / Louisiana.

8 The French passed laws / called the Code Noir, / or "Black Code," / which restricted the ways / in which Africans / in Louisiana could live.

Directions Part C. Turn to page 178 in your Student Edition. Read aloud the first 2 paragraphs three times. Try to improve your reading each time. Record your best time on the lines below.

Number of words	118
My best time	____
Words per minute	____

LA.A.1.2.4(5.1) uses a variety of strategies to monitor reading in fifth-grade or higher level texts (for example, adjusting reading rate according to purpose and text difficulty, rereading, self-correcting, summarizing, checking other sources, class and group discussions, trying an alternate word).

© Harcourt

Name _____ Date _____

Building Vocabulary

Directions Answer the following questions. Use complete sentences.

1 Was *indigo* a *cash crop* in the early southern colony of South Carolina? How did this come to be? _____

_____

2 How did the Calverts provide a *refuge* for Catholics? _____

_____

3 What did Oglethorpe hope to accomplish by bringing *debtors* to Georgia? Why did it not succeed? _____

_____

4 What did the *Puritans* want to do to the Church of England? What did they do instead? _____

_____

5 What kinds of *immigrants* moved to Philadelphia? Why? _____

_____

6 What did the *Fundamental Orders* do for the Connecticut Colony? Why was this important? _____

_____

7 Why do you think that the king gave some British *charters* to settle in the Americas? _____

_____

LA.A.1.2.3(5.1) uses a variety of strategies to determine meaning and increase vocabulary (for example, homonyms, homophones, prefixes, suffixes, word-origins, multiple meanings, antonyms, synonyms, word relationships).
LA.A.2.2.1(5.1) extends previously learned knowledge and skills of fourth grade level with increasingly complex reading texts and assignments and tasks (for example, explicit and implicit ideas).

© Harcourt

FCAT Test Prep

Directions Read the passage "Castillo de San Marcos" before answering Numbers 1 through 8.

Castillo de San Marcos

The Castillo de San Marcos (ka•STEE•yoh day SAN MAR•kohs) is the fort that cannot be taken by force. Completed in 1695, this fort has never been conquered. The English attacked the fort twice, but its walls were so strong that the people inside were not harmed.

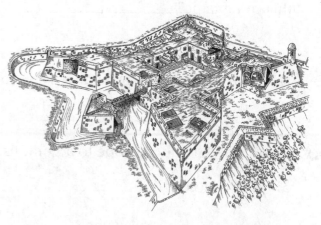

The story of the Castillo de San Marcos began in 1565 when Pedro Menéndez de Avilés (may•NAYN•days day ah•vee•LAYS) and his crew sailed from Spain and reached present-day St. Augustine. They built the first permanent European settlement there. However, their settlement was not much more than a wooden fort. So, English explorer Sir Francis Drake found it easy to attack the fort and destroy it, leaving St. Augustine in ruins. Spain's queen now understood that she must pay for the building of a stone fort that could withstand attack.

Native Floridians, free Africans, slaves, and the Spanish began work on the new fort in 1672. They used a special kind of stone, coquina (koh•KEE•nuh), for the fort. Coquina is a soft yellow limestone, formed of broken shells and coral pressed together underground. It would be strong enough to keep the walls of the fort from being broken.

However, water seeped through the coquina walls, so the rooms were damp. To keep the water from entering through the walls, the outside of the fort was painted white. The painted walls kept the moisture out.

Finally finished in 1695, the fort was named Castillo de San Marcos. It had taken 23 years to build. The walls were 20 feet (6 m) high, 13 feet (4 m) thick at the base, and 9 feet (3 m) thick at the top. If bombarded by cannonballs, the walls would be dented but not broken. Since a water-filled moat surrounded the entire fort, visitors could enter only over a drawbridge. Enemies were unable to break into this strong fort. The Castillo de San Marcos still stands today, the only Spanish structure in Florida that has survived from the 1600s to the present.

Go On ▶

© Harcourt

Directions Now answer Numbers 1 through 8. Base your answers on the passage "Castillo de San Marcos."

1 Why was it so easy for Sir Francis Drake to attack the first fort at St. Augustine?

- Ⓐ The fort was made of stone.
- Ⓑ The fort had coquina walls.
- Ⓒ The fort was made of wood.
- Ⓓ The fort had no drawbridge.

2 Which event occurred FIRST?

- Ⓕ Work began on a new fort.
- Ⓖ The first permanent European settlement was built.
- Ⓗ Spain's queen agreed to pay for the building of a stone fort.
- Ⓘ The English attacked St. Augustine.

3 Coquina was used for the walls of the fort because

- Ⓐ it was strong enough to keep the walls from being broken.
- Ⓑ it allowed water to seep through the walls.
- Ⓒ it was easy to find.
- Ⓓ it is formed of broken shells and coral.

4 All of the following helped build the Castillo de San Marcos EXCEPT

- Ⓕ Native Floridians.
- Ⓖ English explorers.
- Ⓗ the Spanish.
- Ⓘ slaves.

5 Why is the Castillo de San Marcos so important to Florida?

- Ⓐ It is the only fort that the English attacked twice.
- Ⓑ It is the only Spanish structure built with coquina.
- Ⓒ It is the only Spanish structure in Florida that has survived from the 1600s to the present.
- Ⓓ It is the only fort with a water-filled moat and a drawbridge.

6 The Castillo de San Marcos has never been conquered because

- Ⓕ the fort has high walls.
- Ⓖ it was painted white to keep the fort free from moisture.
- Ⓗ the fort cost 138,375 pesos.
- Ⓘ cannonballs fired at the fort cannot destroy the coquina walls.

Go On ▶

© Harcourt

7 READ THINK EXPLAIN The passage says that Spain's queen understood that she would have to pay for the building of a stone fort. Why do you think she was finally willing to do this?

_____

_____

_____

_____

_____

8 READ THINK EXPLAIN It took 23 years to build the Castillo de San Marcos. Write a paragraph that gives some reasons why you think it might have taken so long. Use details from the passage to support your reasons.

_____

_____

_____

_____

_____

_____

STOP

© Harcourt

Name _____ Date _____

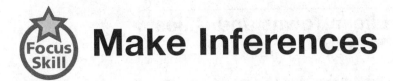

Make Inferences

Directions Read the paragraph below. Then use the information to complete the graphic organizer. Make inferences about crops grown in the middle colonies.

The middle colonies were often called the "breadbasket" colonies. Many of the crops grown there were ones that were used to make bread. These colonies seemed to have everything that was needed for growing crops. The climate, the soil, and other resources of the middle colonies helped the farmers become prosperous. Not only did they grow their own food, but they were also able to sell their surplus crops to other colonies and in Europe.

REMEMBER:
- **When you make an inference, you use facts and your experience to come to a conclusion.**

What I Know

_____

_____

_____

_____

+

What I Read

The middle colonies were called the "breadbasket" colonies. Many of the crops grown there were ones that were used to make bread.

→

Inferences

_____

_____

_____

_____

© Harcourt

LA.A.2.2.1(5.1) extends previously learned knowledge and skills of fourth grade level with increasingly complex reading texts and assignments and tasks (for example, explicit and implicit ideas).
LA.E.2.2.4(5.2) identifies the major information in a nonfiction text.

Lesson 1: Life in Towns and Cities

⭐ Building Text Comprehension
Make Inferences

Directions Read the paragraphs below. Then use the information to complete the graphic organizer on the next page. Base your inferences on what you have read and on what you already know.

The middle colonies welcomed people of different religions. While New Englanders were mainly Puritans, the religions of people living in the middle colonies were varied. These religious groups included Dutch Reformed, Lutherans, Quakers, Anglicans, Dutch Mennonites, French Huguenots, German Baptists, and Portuguese Jews.

Settlers in New Netherland—and later New York, as the English renamed it—included people from the Netherlands, Germany, France, Belgium, and the Scandinavian countries. Each group settled in a different part of New York and

practiced its own religion. By 1771 there were about 18 different places of worship in New York City alone. No wonder New York is still such a diverse place!

New Jersey boasted a variety of religious groups as well. At one time it had 45 different church congregations. William Penn, founder of Pennsylvania, established the Pennsylvania Colony so Quakers could follow their beliefs. He practiced religious tolerance, and people of other religions were encouraged to live in Pennsylvania. At first, Delaware had a diverse religious population. However, over time the Church of England became the major religion.

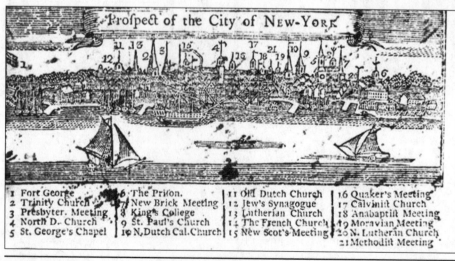

Prospect of the City of New-York

1 Fort George
2 Trinity Church
3 Presbyter. Meeting
4 North D. Church
5 St. George's Chapel
6 The Prison.
7 New Brick Meeting
8 King's College
9 St. Paul's Church
10 N. Dutch Cal. Church
11 Old Dutch Church
12 Jew's Synagogue
13 Lutherian Church
14 The French Church
15 New Scot's Meeting
16 Quaker's Meeting
17 Calvinist Church
18 Anabaptist Meeting
19 Moravian Meeting
20 N. Lutheran Church
21 Methodist Meeting

This woodblock from the late 1700s shows the different places of worship found in New York City.

© Harcourt

(continued)

LA.A.2.2.1(5.1) extends previously learned knowledge and skills of fourth grade level with increasingly complex reading texts and assignments and tasks (for example, explicit and implicit ideas).
LA.E.2.2.4(5.2) identifies the major information in a nonfiction text.

Name _____ Date _____

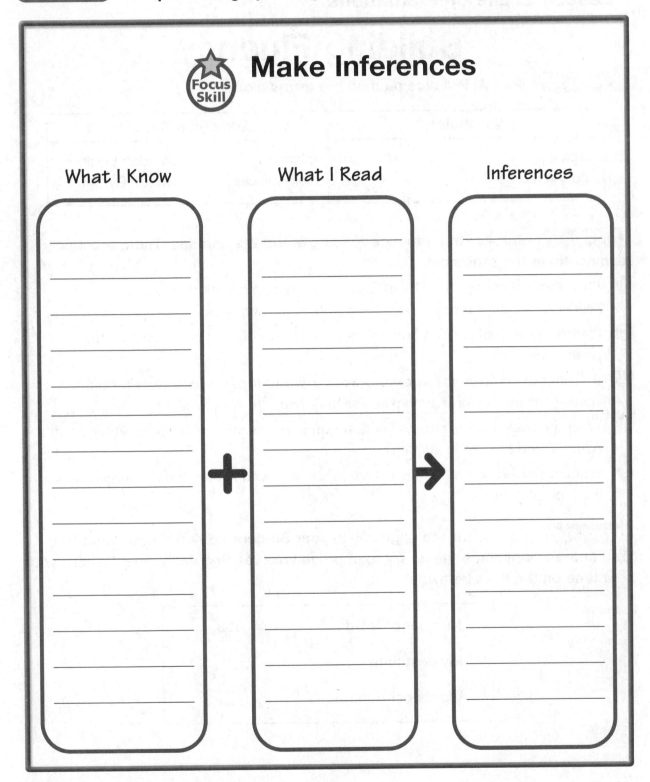

Make Inferences

Focus Skill

What I Know   What I Read   Inferences

+   →

LA.A.2.2.1(5.1) extends previously learned knowledge and skills of fourth grade level with increasingly complex reading texts and assignments and tasks (for example, explicit and implicit ideas).
LA.A.2.2.5(5.1) reads and organizes information from multiple sources for a variety of purposes (for example, supporting opinions, predictions, and conclusions; writing a research report; conducting interviews; taking a test; performing tasks).

© Harcourt

Lesson 2: Life on Plantations

Building Fluency

Directions Part A. Practice reading the terms aloud.

Vocabulary		Additional Terms	
broker	auction	planters	Olaudah Equiano
indentured servant		self-sufficient	William Byrd II

Directions Part B. First, practice reading aloud the phrases. Then, practice reading aloud the sentences.

1 Plantations were mostly self-sufficient, / growing and producing / the much needed food and products / for the planters and workers.

2 Planters used brokers / to buy goods / that they couldn't produce / on their plantations.

3 An indentured servant / agreed to work / without pay / for a certain number of years / for the person / who paid for their trip / to America.

4 When he was 11 years old, / Olaudah Equiano was taken / from his village / in Africa / and sold at an auction.

5 William Byrd II was a planter / from Virginia / who kept a diary / about the harsh life / on plantations.

Directions Part C. Turn to page 200 in your Student Edition. Read aloud the first 2 paragraphs three times. Try to improve your reading each time. Record your best time on the lines below.

Number of words	108
My best time	_____
Words per minute	_____

© Harcourt

LA.A.1.2.4(5.1) uses a variety of strategies to monitor reading in fifth-grade or higher level texts (for example, adjusting reading rate according to purpose and text difficulty, rereading, self-correcting, summarizing, checking other sources, class and group discussions, trying an alternate word).

Lesson 3: Life on the Frontier

Building Vocabulary

Directions Complete each sentence with a term from the box.

backcountry	loft
fall line	coureur de bois

1 A _____ was a part of a house on the frontier located between the ceiling and roof.

2 _____ is a French term that means "runner of the woods."

3 _____ was the land between the Coastal Plain and the Appalachian Mountains in the United States.

4 A _____ is a place where the land drops sharply, causing rivers to form waterfalls.

Directions Answer the following questions.

5 Describe the houses where most people in the backcountry lived. _____

_____

_____

6 Imagine yourself living in the backcountry during the 1700s. What would your life be like? Write a paragraph answering this question to share with classmates.

_____

_____

_____

_____

_____

_____

© Harcourt

LA.A.1.2.3(5.1) uses a variety of strategies to determine meaning and increase vocabulary (for example, homonyms, homophones, prefixes, suffixes, word-origins, multiple meanings, antonyms, synonyms, word relationships).
LA.A.2.2.1(5.1) extends previously learned knowledge and skills of the fourth grade level with increasingly complex reading texts and assignments and tasks (for example, explicit and implicit ideas).

FCAT Test Prep

Directions Read the passage "Fort Mose" before answering Numbers 1 through 7.

Fort Mose

While the English were busy developing the New England, middle, and southern colonies, the Spanish were settling in Florida in St. Augustine. Many free Africans lived in Florida, too.

In 1693 the king of Spain decreed that runaway slaves from the British colonies who came to Florida would be free. These former slaves were required to become Catholics and to declare their loyalty to Spain. Many runaway slaves made their way to freedom and settled in Florida. These freed slaves helped Spanish settlers build the Castillo de San Marcos, the fort at St. Augustine.

In 1738 Florida's governor, Manuel Montiano, established a town for Africans who were free. The town was called Fort Mose (moh•SAY). It was located about 2 miles (3 km) north of St. Augustine. The governor expected that Fort Mose's settlers would be able to grow food for themselves and for the Spanish in St. Augustine. He also expected that the people of Fort Mose would help defend St. Augustine.

Fort Mose became the first town settled by free Africans in North America. The settlers were able to do all that Florida's governor expected of them. They built homes, stores, and churches, and started businesses. The crops they

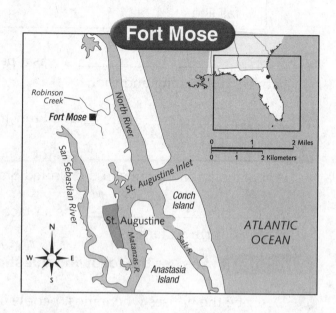

grew provided food for their settlement and for St. Augustine. They followed their African traditions as shown by their dress, crafts, and ways of farming.

The men of Fort Mose formed their own militia under the leadership of Francisco Menendez, a runaway former slave. The militia valiantly fought against James Olgethorpe and the British in 1740. After this attack, the settlers were forced to rebuild much of Fort Mose, and it became harder for the settlement to survive. In 1763, when the British took control of Florida, the settlers of Fort Mose left Florida and headed to Cuba. For the short time it lasted, however, Fort Mose changed the lives of the Africans who lived there.

Go On ▶

Name _____ Date _____

Directions Now answer Numbers 1 through 7. Base your answers on the passage "Fort Mose."

1 Slaves who ran away to Florida became Catholics so that
Ⓐ they would be loyal to England.
Ⓑ they would get away from Southern plantations.
Ⓒ they would fight against the British.
Ⓓ they would be free.

2 How did the freed slaves living in Florida help Spain?
Ⓕ They kept African traditions alive.
Ⓖ They were loyal to England.
Ⓗ They helped build the Castillo de San Marcos.
Ⓘ They went to Cuba.

3 Fort Mose was established by
Ⓐ Francisco Menendez.
Ⓑ Manuel Montiano.
Ⓒ James Oglethorpe.
Ⓓ the king of Spain.

4 What were the settlers of Fort Mose able to do?
Ⓕ keep the British from attacking St. Augustine
Ⓖ teach the Spanish their way of farming
Ⓗ sell their crops to the British colonies
Ⓘ grow enough food for themselves and for the people of St. Augustine

5 Who was Francisco Menendez?
Ⓐ the governor of Florida in 1738
Ⓑ the first runaway slave in Florida
Ⓒ the leader of the Fort Mose militia
Ⓓ the founder of Fort Mose

6 When the British took control of Florida, what happened to the settlers of Fort Mose?
Ⓕ They left Florida and headed to Cuba.
Ⓖ They rebuilt their settlement.
Ⓗ They were returned to their former owners.
Ⓘ They joined the British army.

Go On ▶

FCAT

7 Fort Mose was the first town settled by free Africans in North America. Write a paragraph explaining how this settlement helped both the Africans living there and the Spanish in Florida.

READ
THINK
EXPLAIN

_____

_____

_____

_____

_____

_____

_____

_____

_____

_____

_____

_____

_____

_____

STOP

Name _____   Date _____

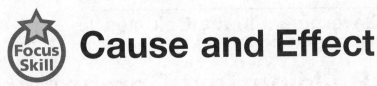

Cause and Effect

Directions Read the paragraphs below. Then use the information to complete the graphic organizer about the French and Indian War and the reason Spain joined the war.

During the mid-1700s, France, Britain, and Spain struggled to keep control of the land they had claimed. France and Britain claimed land east and west of the Ohio Valley. Spain controlled Florida and land south and west of Florida. The French and Indian War broke out because France and Britain each wanted control of the Ohio Valley region.

At first Spain kept out of the war. Eventually, Spain joined the French and their Native American allies against the British. The Spanish did this because they thought that if the British won the war, they would gain control of all of North America.

REMEMBER:

• **A cause is an event or action that makes something else happen.**

• **An effect is what happens as a result of that event or action.**

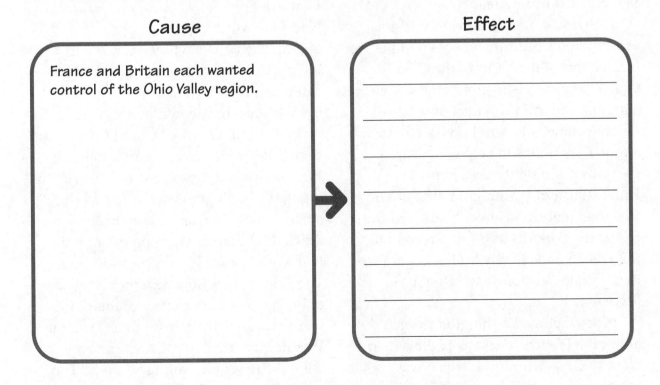

Cause

France and Britain each wanted control of the Ohio Valley region.

Effect

LA.A.2.2.1(5.1) extends previously learned knowledge and skills of the fourth grade level with increasingly complex reading texts and assignments and tasks (for example, explicit and implicit ideas).
LA.E.2.2.1(5.1) understands cause-and-effect relationships in literary texts.

© Harcourt

Name _____   Date _____

Building Text Comprehension
Cause and Effect

Directions Read the paragraphs below. Then complete the graphic organizer on the next page. Use what you have read to identify the causes and effects of the actions of George Washington, the French, and the British.

George Washington was 21 years old when he was given the job of telling the French to leave the Ohio Valley. Robert Dinwiddie of Virginia sent George Washington across the Appalachians with a warning to the French that they must stop moving into British territory. The French, of course, had no intention of leaving, and they told Washington that. He returned to Virginia.

Dinwiddie, not wanting to wait for Washington's return, sent some soldiers to build a fort at the Forks of the Ohio River. When George Washington returned to Virginia, Dinwiddie made him a lieutenant colonel and sent him back with about 400 soldiers to help the group that was building the fort. However, Dinwiddie and Washington did not know that the French had already attacked the fort at the Forks of the Ohio River. In fact, the French had already built a larger fort in the same location—Fort Duquesne (doo•KAYN).

When George Washington learned about the French attack, he and his men went to Great Meadows, which was southeast of Fort Duquesne. Here they

George Washington

built their own fort—Fort Necessity. They hoped to be prepared for any French attack. An Indian friend informed Washington that French soldiers were on their way to attack Fort Necessity. Washington and his men attacked the French party, killing 10 of them, wounding 1, and capturing 21.

The French, angered by this attack, waited about two months and then fought back. The French forces, outnumbering Washington's troops, were so overwhelming that Washington was forced to surrender. Since war had not been officially declared, Washington and his men were allowed to return to Virginia. The British were now convinced that the only way to regain control of their land was to wage war against France. George Washington's actions against the French were the first of his military career. They led to the French and Indian War.

(continued)

LA.A.2.2.1(5.1) extends previously learned knowledge and skills of the fourth grade level with increasingly complex reading texts and assignments and tasks (for example, explicit and implicit ideas).
LA.E.2.2.1(5.1) understands cause-and-effect relationships in literary texts.

© Harcourt

Name _____ Date _____

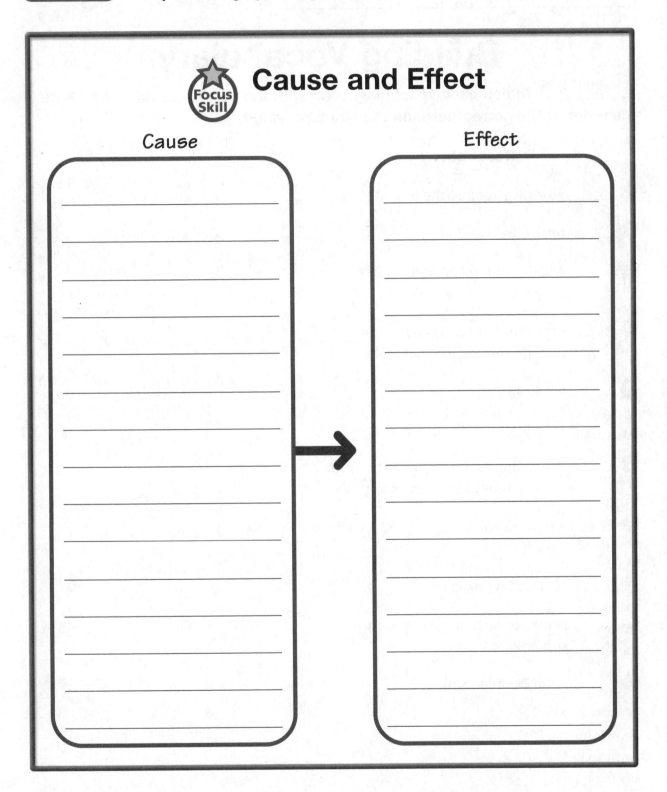

Cause and Effect

Cause

Effect

LA.A.2.2.1(5.1) extends previously learned knowledge and skills of the fourth grade level with increasingly complex reading texts and assignments and tasks (for example, explicit and implicit ideas).
LA.E.2.2.1(5.1) understands cause-and-effect relationships in literary texts.

Lesson 2: Quarrels and Conflicts

Building Vocabulary

Directions Match each vocabulary term with the correct description. Write the letter of the correct term on the blank provided.

Description   **Term**

1 _____ working against the government   **A.** tariff

2 _____ refuse to buy   **B.** Loyalists

3 _____ a tax on goods brought into a   **C.** representation
             country
                                                      D. treason
4 _____ a meeting of representatives who
             have authority to make decisions   **E.** public opinion

5 _____ freedom   **F.** petition

6 _____ Tories   **G.** liberty

7 _____ the killing of a number of people   **H.** boycott
             who cannot defend themselves
                                                      I. congress
8 _____ a request for action signed by many
             people   **J.** repeal

9 _____ undo a law or tax   **K.** massacre

10 _____ acting or speaking on behalf of
             someone

11 _____ what people think

LA.A.1.2.3(5.4) uses resources and references such as dictionary, thesaurus, and context to build word meanings.
LA.A.1.2.3(5.5) identifies, classifies, and demonstrates knowledge of levels of specificity among fifth-grade or higher level words from a variety of categories.

Lesson 3: Colonists Unite

Building Fluency

Directions Part A. Practice reading the terms aloud.

Vocabulary		Additional Terms
Committee of Correspondence consequences blockade quarter	Continental Congress rights Minuteman Patriot	Intolerable Acts Lexington Concord

Directions Part B. First, practice reading aloud the phrases. Then, practice reading aloud the sentences.

1 Samuel Adams / set up a Committee of Correspondence.

2 The colonists knew / that their actions / would have major consequences.

3 British Parliament ordered the Navy / to blockade Boston Harbor.

4 The British also ordered the colonists / to quarter British soldiers, / a law that became part of / the Intolerable Acts.

5 Representatives from almost every colony / met at the Continental Congress.

6 The colonists believed / that they had rights.

7 Members of Massachusetts colony's militia / became known as Minutemen.

8 A Patriot was a colonist / who was against / British rule.

9 British General Thomas Gage / sent troops / into Lexington and Concord / to find weapons.

Directions Part C. Turn to page 238 in your Student Edition. Read aloud the first 2 paragraphs three times. Try to improve your reading each time. Record your best time on the lines below.

Number of words	112
My best time	____
Words per minute	____

LA.A.1.2.4(5.1) uses a variety of strategies to monitor reading in fifth-grade or higher level texts (for example, adjusting reading rate according to purpose and text difficulty, rereading, self-correcting, summarizing, checking other sources, class and group discussions, trying an alternate word).

FCAT Test Prep

Directions Read the passage "The New Smyrna Colony" before answering Numbers 1 through 7.

The New Smyrna Colony

After the French and Indian War, Florida became a British colony. The British divided Florida into two parts—East Florida and West Florida. The capital of East Florida was St. Augustine, and the capital of West Florida was Pensacola. To encourage settlement in Florida, the British offered settlers land grants. More land could also be purchased from the government at a low price.

Dr. Andrew Turnbull from Scotland took advantage of the grants and organized a colony called New Smyrna (SMEHR•nuh) in 1768. Named after his wife's birthplace, Smyrna, Greece, the colony was even larger than the Jamestown Colony. Turnbull gathered people from Greece, Italy, and the island of Minorca (mih•NAWR•kuh) to come to New Smyrna. In all, about 1,400 people came with him.

Many of these people agreed to be indentured servants so that after six years they could receive 50 acres of land. When the settlers arrived in New Smyrna, which was about 80 miles (129 km) south of St. Augustine, all the land had to be cleared. Turnbull did not even have enough food for the entire group. During the first three years, many people died.

Between 1771 and 1777, however, indigo and other crops were exported, and the colony seemed to be thriving. Turnbull

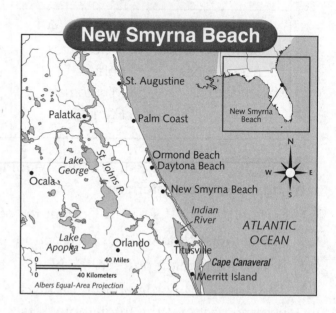

New Smyrna Beach

had ideas to help the colony continue to grow. He had the colonists build a system of canals similar to the Egyptian irrigation system of canals. This system was new to North America. It turned swamps into fertile land, provided transportation, and gave the colonists water.

In spite of the improvements, most of the workers were unhappy. Turnbull's overseers did nothing to help them and were often cruel and abusive. Many workers went to St. Augustine and asked the governor for help. He freed them and provided homes for them in St. Augustine. Most of the other New Smyrna colonists also left and settled in St. Augustine. Thus, the New Smyrna Colony failed. Today the city of New Smyrna Beach is on land that was once part of the original colony.

Go On ▶

© Harcourt

Name _____ Date _____

Directions Now answer Numbers 1 through 7. Base your answers on the passage "The New Smyrna Colony."

1 The MAIN purpose of British land grants was to
   Ⓐ encourage the planting and harvesting of crops.
   Ⓑ build large plantations and provide work to people.
   Ⓒ encourage people to settle in Florida.
   Ⓓ create a system of canals.

2 People came to the New Smyrna Colony from all of the following places EXCEPT
   Ⓕ Italy.
   Ⓖ France.
   Ⓗ Greece.
   Ⓘ Minorca.

3 Where was the New Smyrna Colony located?
   Ⓐ east of St. Augustine
   Ⓑ west of St. Augustine
   Ⓒ north of St. Augustine
   Ⓓ south of St. Augustine

4 What did Turnbull make the colonists do?
   Ⓕ build a system of canals
   Ⓖ return to their native lands
   Ⓗ build a fort for protection
   Ⓘ grow enough food for all of East Florida

5 Many of the people who came to the New Smyrna Colony were
   Ⓐ indentured servants.
   Ⓑ slaves.
   Ⓒ free people.
   Ⓓ British.

6 What happened to the New Smyrna Colony?
   Ⓕ It became a leading exporter of indigo.
   Ⓖ It was made the capital of East Florida.
   Ⓗ It became the city of New Smyrna Beach.
   Ⓘ It failed because most of the colonists left.

Go On ▶

© Harcourt

7 **READ THINK EXPLAIN** Andrew Turnbull formed the New Smyrna Colony and used ideas from other civilizations to make the colony grow. Write a paragraph describing the colony, Turnbull's ideas, and the reason the colony ended up failing. Use details from the passage in your paragraph.

_____

_____

_____

_____

_____

_____

_____

_____

_____

_____

_____

_____

_____

_____

_____

STOP

Name _____   Date _____

Focus Skill

Sequence

Directions Read the paragraph below. Then use the information to complete the graphic organizer about Britain, its colonies, and the beginning of independence for the colonies.

After the French and Indian War, Britain had a huge debt. To help pay off the cost of the war, Britain placed taxes on the colonies. Many colonists were angry about the taxes and did not want the British to rule them anymore. In April 1775, fighting broke out in Massachusetts between British soldiers and colonists who did not want British rule. Other battles followed. Leaders from the colonies met, and on July 4, 1776, they signed the Declaration of Independence, which stated that the colonies were now separate from Britain. A new country was born—the United States of America.

REMEMBER:
• A sequence is the order in which events occur.

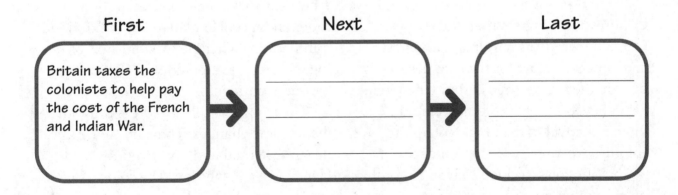

First
Britain taxes the colonists to help pay the cost of the French and Indian War.

Next

Last

LA.A.2.2.1(5.1) extends previously learned knowledge and skills of the fourth grade level with increasingly complex reading texts and assignments and tasks (for example, explicit and implicit ideas).
LA.E.2.2.4(5.2) identifies the major information in a nonfiction text.

Lesson 1: At War with the Homeland

Building Text Comprehension
Sequence

Directions Read the paragraphs below. Then use the information to complete the graphic organizer on the next page.

It took months for the colonies to agree that independence from Britain was best. Specific people and events helped change the colonists' ideas and finally led to independence.

In January 1776, *Common Sense* by Thomas Paine was published. In this pamphlet Paine urged people to seek independence from Britain. Many people, including George Washington and Thomas Jefferson, read this pamphlet. It had a great influence on the colonists.

In June of the same year, the Second Continental Congress met. Richard Henry Lee, who was from Virginia, presented a resolution calling for the colonies to declare themselves free and independent. He believed that the colonies should no longer be loyal to the king. Not all the colonies were ready for such a decision. So the Congress decided to wait a month before voting on such an important issue.

The Congress did, however, choose a committee to write a draft declaring its views on independence. Benjamin Franklin, John Adams, Robert Livingston, Roger Sherman, and Thomas Jefferson

were all part of this committee. The committee selected Thomas Jefferson to write the draft. Members added some ideas, but Jefferson was responsible for the writing. For 17 nights Thomas Jefferson crafted

Richard Henry Lee

what was to become the Declaration of Independence. He planned it and divided it into parts. When he was finished writing, Jefferson presented the work to the Second Continental Congress.

The Congress discussed the draft and made some changes. Then, on July 2, the delegates voted and approved Richard Henry Lee's resolution. The colonies were ready to break their ties with Britain and become free and independent. Two days later, on July 4, the Congress approved the Declaration of Independence, and the 13 colonies became the United States of America.

(continued)

LA.A.2.2.1(5.1) extends previously learned knowledge and skills of the fourth grade level with increasingly complex reading texts and assignments and tasks (for example, explicit and implicit ideas).
LA.E.2.2.4(5.2) identifies the major information in a nonfiction text.

© Harcourt

Name _____ Date _____

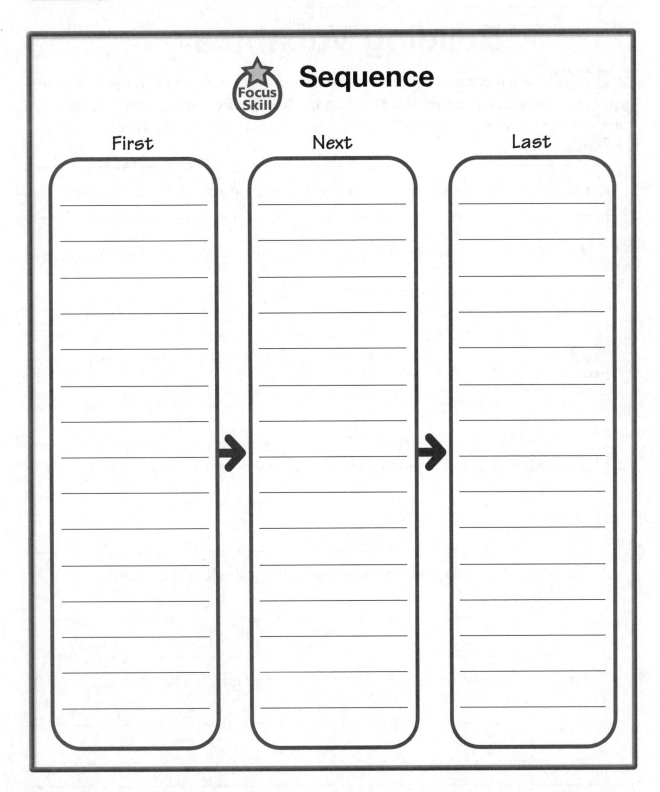

Sequence

Focus Skill

First

Next

Last

LA.A.2.2.1(5.1) extends previously learned knowledge and skills of the fourth grade level with increasingly complex reading texts and assignments and tasks (for example, explicit and implicit ideas).
LA.E.2.2.4(5.2) identifies the major information in a nonfiction text.

© Harcourt

Name _____   Date _____

Building Vocabulary

Directions Each vocabulary term is found in a sentence below. If the use of the term in the sentence is correct, write *C* on the line before the sentence number. If the use is not correct, write *NC* on the line and then rewrite the sentence so it is correct.

revolution	independence	allegiance	declaration	grievance

_____ **1** The committee wrote a revolution stating that the colonies were cutting their

ties with the British government. _____

_____

_____ **2** Many colonists wanted to be independent, or free to govern on their own.

_____

_____

_____ **3** Richard Henry Lee felt that the colonies did not owe allegiance to the king.

_____

_____

_____ **4** In *Common Sense,* Thomas Paine asked the colonies to start a declaration.

_____

_____

_____ **5** The colonists wrote a list of grievances, or praises, against the king.

_____

_____

LA.A.1.2.3(5.1) uses a variety of strategies to determine meaning and increase vocabulary (for example, homonyms, homophones, prefixes, suffixes, word-origins, multiple meanings, antonyms, synonyms, word relationships).
LA.A.2.2.1(5.1) extends previously learned knowledge and skills of the fourth grade level with increasingly complex reading texts and assignments and tasks (for example, explicit and implicit ideas).

© Harcourt

Name _____   Date _____

Reading Biographies

Directions Read the passage about Mercy Otis Warren. Then use what you have learned to answer the question below.

Mercy Otis Warren
Character Trait: Responsibility

Mercy Otis Warren was born in Massachusetts in 1728. As a child, she was known for sharing her feelings and ideas through writing. She also was very outspoken about the politics of the time.

In 1754 she married James Warren and went to live in Plymouth, Massachusetts. After her youngest son was born, Warren began to publish her writings. Her first work appeared in the *Massachusetts Spy*. Much of her writing had to do with Britain's unfairness to the colonists. Warren supported the Patriot cause and believed that she had a responsibility to share her ideas with the colonists. She wanted them to know that no one in the colonies could afford the taxes imposed on British goods. She wanted them to know that women should have rights, too, and that the colonies would be better off if they were independent from Britain.

In two of her plays, Warren challenged the ideas of the Loyalists. She believed that the British could never understand what the colonists wanted and needed. Her writings clearly supported the idea of independence and freedom from Britain. Warren also felt that women had few rights under British rule. She often wrote about women heroes and the problems women had in other countries.

After the Revolutionary War ended, Warren wrote a history of the American Revolution. It was the first book of its kind to be written by a woman.

Warren died in Plymouth in 1814. She will always be remembered for speaking out about her ideas on independence and women's rights and for supporting the Patriots.

1 Mercy Otis Warren felt that it was her **responsibility** to share her ideas about independence. How did she use writing to fulfill this **responsibility**?

_____

_____

LA.A.2.2.1(5.1) extends previously learned knowledge and skills of the fourth grade level with increasingly complex reading texts and assignments and tasks (for example, explicit and implicit ideas).
LA.E.1.2.1(5.3) reads a variety of literary and informational texts (for example, fiction, drama, poetry, myths, fantasies, historical fiction, biographies, autobiographies, textbooks, manuals, magazines).

© Harcourt

Lesson 4: *Samuel's Choice*

Building Fluency

Directions Part A. Practice reading the terms aloud.

Vocabulary	
Samuel Abraham	buoys
Major Mordecai Gist	bailing
freedom bread	

Directions Part B. First, practice reading aloud the phrases. Then, practice reading aloud the sentences.

1 Samuel Abraham was a slave / in Brooklyn / during the Revolutionary War / who decided / to help the Patriots / rather than the British.

2 After Sana found Samuel, / she gave him / some freedom bread / to eat.

3 Samuel helped Major Mordecai Gist / and George Washington's troops / by setting up a rope / to guide the Patriots / against the wind and current.

4 Samuel also put buoys / on the rope / so that it would float.

5 When the boat / that Samuel was sailing / started to fill up / with water, / Sana began bailing out the water.

Directions Part C. Turn to page 260 in your Student Edition. Read aloud the first 2 paragraphs three times. Try to improve your reading each time. Record your best time on the lines below.

Number of words	98
My best time	_____
Words per minute	_____

© Harcourt

LA.A.1.2.4(5.1) uses a variety of strategies to monitor reading in fifth-grade or higher level texts (for example, adjusting reading rate according to purpose and text difficulty, rereading, self-correcting, summarizing, checking other sources, class and group discussions, trying an alternate word).

Lesson 5: Victory and Independence

Reading Primary Sources

Directions The entries below are from the journal of British Major Robert Farmar. He was at the Battle of Pensacola. Pensacola was the capital of West Florida, so it was under British control. Spain, however, joined the war as an ally of France. After you have read the entries, use them to answer the questions.

1781 Friday March 9th. Appeared in sight a Spanish fleet consisting of 32 sails of vessels. The same night they landed a number of men on St. Rose Island.
Sunday 11th. The enemy erected [built] batteries on Rose Island which obliged [caused] the *Mentor* and *Port Royal* to quit their station.
Saturday 31st. The enemy encamped in Neil's Meadow.
Monday 2d. . . . The enemy this evening embarked [boarded] all their troops.
Wednesday 4th. Last night the enemy took possession of the Port Royal. . . .
Wednesday 2d. May. About 9 o'clock this morning the enemy hoisted their flag & open batteries of 6 24 lb and 2 mortars. . . .
Tuesday 8th May. About 9 o'clock a.m. a shell from the enemy's front battery was thrown in at the door of the Magazine . . . which blew it up and killed forty seamen belonging to H.M. ships the *Mentor* & *Port Royal* & forty-five men of the Pennsylvania Loyalists were killed by the same explosion—there were a number of men wounded besides. . . . About 2 o'clock p.m. hoisted a flag of truce from Fort George, & offered to surrender upon capitulation.
Thursday 10th. About 5 o'clock p.m. we surrendered to the arms of Spain.

---

1 What happened on March 9, 1781? _____

2 What did the Spanish do on March 11? _____

_____

3 Reread the entries for March 31 and April 2 and 4. Write a sentence that best describes what the Spanish did on those days.

_____

4 On May 8, what happened at about 9 o'clock? At about 2 o'clock?

_____

5 When did the Spanish finally take control of Pensacola? _____

LA.E.1.2.1(5.3) reads a variety of literary and informational texts (for example, fiction, drama, poetry, myths, fantasies, historical fiction, biographies, autobiographies, textbooks, manuals, magazines).
LA.E.2.2.4(5.2) identifies the major information in a nonfiction text.

Name _____   Date _____

FCAT Test Prep

Directions Read the passage "Florida and the Revolutionary War" before answering Numbers 1 through 8.

Florida and the Revolutionary War

At the start of the Revolutionary War, East Florida and West Florida were under British control. However, the people of Florida did not have the same problems with the British that other colonists did because the British had ruled them for less than 20 years. Most Floridians were Loyalists, people who supported Britain.

The people of Florida did not want the war to reach them, but that was not to be. First, Britain decided to use Florida as a training ground for the troops that would be fighting in the southern colonies. Then, the British turned the Castillo de San Marcos in St. Augustine into a prison camp. The British also expected Floridians to make supplies their military would need.

Two battles were fought in Florida. One battle was between the Americans and the British, and the other battle was between the British and the Spanish. The Battle of Thomas Creek was fought in 1777 near present-day Jacksonville. It was a battle between the Continental Army and the British army. The British had been raiding parts of Georgia, using Florida as a base. Colonel John Baker led about 100 troops into Florida to stop these raids. Colonel Samuel Elbert and his Continental Army of about 400 troops were supposed to join Baker to help take control of St. Augustine. However, before Elbert's troops joined Baker's troops, the British, the East Florida Rangers, and the Creek Indians attacked Baker's troops. The Americans were no match for Britain and its allies, and they were forced to retreat from Florida.

The Battle of Pensacola was fought between the British and the Spanish in Florida. However, the Spanish did not enter the war in order to help the Americans, though they ended up doing just that. Bernardo de Gálvez, the governor of Spanish Louisiana, was determined to retake West Florida for Spain.

Taking Pensacola, in West Florida, proved to be difficult for Gálvez and his troops. The British forces were more numerous than Gálvez's, and Britain had Native American allies. For about two months, the Spanish fired on Pensacola. Then they blew up the British supply of gunpowder, destroying the part of the fort that protected Pensacola. The British were forced to surrender. Spain once again had control of West Florida. The British stronghold in Florida was weakened, which greatly helped the Americans.

Bernardo de Gálvez

© Harcourt

Go On ▶

FCAT

Directions Now answer Numbers 1 through 8. Base your answers on the passage "Florida and the Revolutionary War."

1 At the start of the Revolutionary War, which country controlled East Florida and West Florida?
Ⓐ Spain
Ⓑ France
Ⓒ Britain
Ⓓ the United States

2 A Loyalist was
Ⓕ a person who did not want British rule.
Ⓖ a person who supported Britain.
Ⓗ a person who supported Spain.
Ⓘ a person who worked for another person without pay.

3 How did the British defeat the Continental Army at Thomas Creek?
Ⓐ by attacking Baker's Patriots before they were joined by the rest of the Continental Army
Ⓑ by raiding forts in Georgia
Ⓒ by attacking Elbert's men
Ⓓ by joining forces with the Spanish

4 What did Bernardo de Gálvez hope to do?
Ⓕ help the Continental Army win the Revolutionary War
Ⓖ keep the Continental Army from taking control of Florida
Ⓗ retake West Florida for Spain
Ⓘ protect Spain's holdings in Florida

5 Which statement is FALSE?
Ⓐ The people of Florida did not want to be involved in the Revolutionary War.
Ⓑ The people of Florida did not support the other colonists.
Ⓒ Most of the people of Florida wanted the British to win the Revolutionary War.
Ⓓ The people of Florida wanted to be involved in the Revolutionary War.

6 Why was the Battle of Pensacola important to Spain?
Ⓕ Spain regained control of West Florida.
Ⓖ It guaranteed the British would lose the war.
Ⓗ It provided Spain with holdings in North America.
Ⓘ It meant the Americans had to retreat from Florida.

© Harcourt

Go On ▶

FCAT

7 Many people living in Florida wanted Britain to win the Revolutionary War. Why do you think this was so?

READ
THINK
EXPLAIN

_____

_____

_____

_____

_____

_____

_____

_____

8 How were Spain's actions in Florida in the Revolutionary War helpful to the Continental Army?

READ
THINK
EXPLAIN

_____

_____

_____

_____

_____

_____

_____

_____

Name _____ Date _____

 # Summarize

Directions Read the paragraph below. Then use the information to complete the graphic organizer about Continentals.

To pay for the Revolutionary War, Congress began printing and coining money. This money was called Continentals. Benjamin Franklin and other members of Congress came up with a design for both the paper money and coins. This design had a sundial and sun with the words *The United Colonies*. Congress caused inflation to occur by printing too much money. Since the money had very little value, people started using the expression "Not worth a Continental" to describe things that were basically worthless.

REMEMBER:
* **When you summarize, you give a shortened version of what you have read.**

Facts

What?   Paper money and coins
Who?   Continental Congress
Where? 13 colonies
How?   Printed too much money
             and caused inflation
Why?   To pay for the Revolutionary War

Summary

_____

_____

_____

_____

_____

_____

LA.A.1.2.4(5.1) uses a variety of strategies to monitor reading in fifth-grade or higher level texts (for example, adjusting reading rate according to purpose and text difficulty, rereading, self-correcting, summarizing, checking other sources, class and group discussions, trying an alternate word).
LA.A.2.2.1(5.1) extends previously learned knowledge and skills of the fourth grade level with increasingly complex reading texts and assignments and tasks (for example, explicit and implicit ideas).
LA.E.2.2.4(5.2) identifies the major information in a nonfiction text.

Lesson 1: The Articles of Confederation

⭐ Building Text Comprehension
Focus Skill
Summarize

Directions Read the passage below about the Northwest Ordinance. Then use the information from the passage to complete the graphic organizer on the next page.

The United States Congress passed the Northwest Ordinance in 1787. This ordinance, or set of laws, set up a plan for governing the Northwest Territory, which included lands north of the Ohio River. The Northwest Ordinance outlined the steps that must be followed for new states to be formed from the Northwest Territory. There were three stages a territory had to go through to become a state.

In the first stage, Congress chose the leaders of the territory. These leaders were a governor, a secretary, and three judges. Each one of them had to own land and live in the territory. The governor and the judges selected laws for the territory from laws that were used by existing states. Congress had to approve these selected laws.

The second stage occurred when at least 5,000 free men had settled in the territory. These free men were then allowed to elect a legislature. However, only adult males who owned at least 50 acres of land were allowed to vote. The legislature consisted of a house of representatives and a legislative council.

In the third stage, a territory with a population of at least 60,000 people was ready to become a state. The territory's leaders had to write a state constitution. The document would then be sent to the United States Congress for its approval. The ordinance required that slavery not be allowed in states that were formed from the Northwest Territory.

The Northwest Ordinance led to the formation of the states of Ohio, Indiana, Illinois, Michigan, and Wisconsin. It also set the guidelines for other territories hoping for statehood.

(continued)

Conestoga wagon, often used by settlers moving to the Northwest Territory

© Harcourt

LA.A.1.2.4(5.1) uses a variety of strategies to monitor reading in fifth-grade or higher level texts (for example, adjusting reading rate according to purpose and text difficulty, rereading, self-correcting, summarizing, checking other sources, class and group discussions, trying an alternate word).
LA.A.2.2.1(5.1) extends previously learned knowledge and skills of the fourth grade level with increasingly complex reading texts and assignments and tasks (for example, explicit and implicit ideas).
LA.E.2.2.4(5.2) identifies the major information in a nonfiction text.

Name _____ Date _____

Directions **Complete the graphic organizer.**

Focus Skill

Summarize

Facts   Summary

→

LA.A.1.2.4(5.1) uses a variety of strategies to monitor reading in fifth-grade or higher level texts (for example, adjusting reading rate according to purpose and text difficulty, rereading, self-correcting, summarizing, checking other sources, class and group discussions, trying an alternate word).
LA.A.2.2.1(5.1) extends previously learned knowledge and skills of the fourth grade level with increasingly complex reading texts and assignments and tasks (for example, explicit and implicit ideas).
LA.E.2.2.4(5.2) identifies the major information in a nonfiction text.

© Harcourt

Reading Support for Social Studies

Name _____ Date _____

Reading Biographies

Directions Read the passage about Gouverneur Morris. Use what you have learned to answer the questions below.

Gouverneur Morris
Character Trait: Patriotism

Gouverneur (guh•ver•NIR) Morris was born in 1752 in Westchester County, New York. Although most members of his family were Loyalists, Morris supported the colonists who were angry with Britain. In 1775 Morris was elected to New York's congress, and in 1776 he helped write a draft of New York's constitution. By 1778 he was a member of the Continental Congress. Morris signed the Articles of Confederation and was actively involved in writing the draft of a treaty to end the Revolutionary War.

Later, Morris became involved in the Constitutional Convention. His most important job was to record the ideas that had been approved during the convention and to determine the best wording for the Constitution.

Originally the wording for the Preamble to the Constitution had been "We the people of the States of New Hampshire, Massachusetts, . . . " Morris changed the words to "We the people of the United States . . ." because he believed the people needed to know that they were citizens of the United States first and then citizens of their individual states. He continued making changes to the wording until it was clear to all who read it that the Constitution guaranteed that citizens would be treated fairly and would always be free.

Morris later served as a minister to France and as a senator. He died in 1816, after having spent most of his life in service to the United States.

1 What was Morris's most important job at the Constitutional Convention?

_____

2 How is Morris an example of the character trait **patriotism**? _____

_____

© Harcourt

LA.E.1.2.1(5.3) reads a variety of informational texts (for example, fiction, drama, poetry, myths, fantasies, historical fiction, biographies, autobiographies, textbooks, manuals, magazines).
LA.E.1.2.2(5.3) makes inferences and draws conclusions regarding story elements of a fifth grade or higher level text (for example, the traits, actions, and motives of characters; plot development; setting).

Name _____ Date _____

Reading Charts and Graphs

Directions Use the chart about the Articles of Confederation, the Great Compromise/Constitution, and the Virginia Plan to answer the questions.

Articles of Confederation	Great Compromise/ Constitution	Virginia Plan
National government is made up of Congress.	National government has three branches—legislative, executive, and judicial.	National government has three branches—legislative, executive, and judicial.
State governments are represented equally in Congress.	Congress is divided into two houses. Representation in one house is based on population of each state. Representation in the other house is equal for all states.	States with greater populations have more representatives and more votes in Congress.
National government has no veto power over states.	National government has no veto power over states.	National government has veto power over states.
State governments have more power than national government.	Power is divided between national and state governments as specified by the Constitution.	National government has more power than state governments.

1 Which plan gives states with greater populations more representation?

_____

2 According to the Articles of Confederation, which has more power, the national

government or the governments of individual states? _____

3 Under the Great Compromise/Constitution, how would Congress be organized?

_____

LA.A.2.2.1(5.1) extends previously learned knowledge and skills of the fourth grade level with increasingly complex reading texts and assignments and tasks (for example, explicit and implicit ideas).
LA.A.2.2.5(5.1) reads and organizes information from multiple sources for a variety of purposes (for example, supporting opinions, predictions, and conclusions; writing a research report; conducting interviews; taking a test; performing tasks).

© Harcourt

Lesson 4: A Government of Three Branches

Building Vocabulary

Directions Match each vocabulary term with the correct description. Write the letter of the correct term on the blank provided.

Description	Term
1 _____ does not follow the constitution	**A.** legislative branch
2 _____ judges	**B.** executive branch
3 _____ reject bills	**C.** judicial branch
4 _____ the greater part	**D.** separation of powers
5 _____ makes the laws	**E.** majority
6 _____ oversees carrying out the laws	**F.** census
7 _____ a population count	**G.** electoral college
8 _____ a group of electors	**H.** veto
9 _____ to accuse a government official of wrongdoing	**I.** impeach
	J. justices
10 _____ keep one branch of government from using its authority wrongly	**K.** override
11 _____ a vote to cancel	**L.** unconstitutional
12 _____ settles differences about the meaning of the laws	**M.** checks and balances
13 _____ division of the national government	

LA.A.1.2.3(5.4) uses resources and references such as dictionary, thesaurus, and context to build word meanings.
LA.A.1.2.3(5.5) identifies, classifies, and demonstrates knowledge of levels of specificity among fifth-grade or higher level words from a variety of categories.

© Harcourt

Name _____ Date _____

Building Fluency

Directions Part A. Practice reading the terms aloud.

Vocabulary	
formulate	stoic
unanimous	advocating
subscribed	meticulously
surmises	infallibility

Directions Part B. First, practice reading aloud the phrases. Then, practice reading aloud the sentences.

1 The delegates / to the Constitutional Convention / worked to formulate / a document / that would please everyone.

2 The states wanted / to be unanimous / in their decision / to sign the Constitution.

3 Throughout the story, / Jared surmises what will happen next / during the meeting.

4 George Washington's face / remained a very stoic one / throughout the Constitutional Convention.

5 Alexander Hamilton / wrote many articles and papers / advocating a strong federal government.

6 The delegates / worked meticulously / on the Constitution.

7 Benjamin Franklin / spoke during the meeting, / informing everyone of his doubt, / concerning his own infallibility.

8 All but 16 of the 55 delegates / subscribed their names / on the new / United States Constitution.

Directions Part C. Turn to page 306 in your Student Edition. Read aloud the first 2 paragraphs three times. Try to improve your reading each time. Record your best time on the lines below.

Number of words	119
My best time	_____
Words per minute	_____

LA.A.1.2.4(5.1) uses a variety of strategies to monitor reading in fifth-grade or higher level texts (for example, adjusting reading rate according to purpose and text difficulty, rereading, self-correcting, summarizing, checking other sources, class and group discussions, trying an alternate word).

FCAT Test Prep

Directions Read the passage "Franklin's Necessary Inventions" before answering Numbers 1 through 8.

Franklin's Necessary Inventions

There's an old saying, "Necessity is the mother of invention." Certainly that is how many of Benjamin Franklin's inventions came to be. Bifocals, for example, came about because of Franklin's vision problem. When he read, he needed glasses, and he did not like having to take them off when he wanted to see things that were far away. So he devised a pair of glasses that would allow him to see both near and far. He cut two pairs of glasses in half and then put half of each lens in one glass frame. That meant that when he looked through part of the lens he could see near and when he looked through the other part he could see far. Today, bifocals are used by millions of people for the same reason.

Another invention of Franklin's was a furnace called a Franklin stove. During his lifetime—the 1700s—people kept their houses warm by building a fire in the fireplace. Not only was a lot of wood needed to do this, but it was dangerous, since homes could catch on fire. The Franklin stove provided a safer way to keep houses warm. Today, although most houses are heated with electricity, others still use a modern version of the furnace for heat.

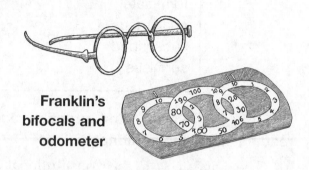

Franklin's bifocals and odometer

The odometer was another of Franklin's inventions. Franklin served as a postmaster for the colonies. He was responsible for determining routes and measuring distances for carrying the mail. He did not have any way to measure these distances. So, he came up with the idea of a tool that could measure these distances and keep track of them. He placed his invention on his carriage. Today, cars and other vehicles have odometers that keep track of distance traveled.

Some of Franklin's other inventions include the lightning rod, a waterproof bulkhead for ships, and a tool for reaching books on high shelves. In addition to his inventions, Franklin also established some services for the people of the American colonies. These included a newspaper, an almanac, a library, a fire department, a voluntary army, and a hospital.

Go On ▶

© Harcourt

Directions Now answer Numbers 1 through 8. Base your answers on the passage "Franklin's Necessary Inventions."

1 Which statement is the BEST summary for this passage?

Ⓐ Benjamin Franklin's inventions helped keep people safe.

Ⓑ Many of Benjamin Franklin's inventions came about because he needed to solve a problem.

Ⓒ All Benjamin Franklin's inventions involved electricity.

Ⓓ Benjamin Franklin's inventions are all used today.

2 Benjamin Franklin invented bifocals so he could

Ⓕ see far.

Ⓖ see near.

Ⓗ see both near and far.

Ⓘ see without glasses.

3 Why was the Franklin stove a necessary invention?

Ⓐ It used a lot of wood to heat houses.

Ⓑ It meant houses could no longer catch on fire.

Ⓒ It was cheaper to use than electricity.

Ⓓ It provided people with a safer way to heat their houses.

4 What is a tool for measuring and recording distances?

Ⓕ an odometer

Ⓖ a bifocal

Ⓗ a bulkhead

Ⓘ a speedometer

5 Benjamin Franklin most likely invented the lightning rod so

Ⓐ houses and other buildings would not be damaged if they were struck by lightning.

Ⓑ he could prove that lightning is a form of electricity.

Ⓒ he could see if lightning strikes would cause damage to houses.

Ⓓ other scientists would experiment with electricity.

6 According to the passage, Benjamin Franklin established all the following services EXCEPT

Ⓕ a fire department.

Ⓖ a library.

Ⓗ a police department.

Ⓘ a hospital.

Go On ▶

FCAT

7 Read the saying "Necessity is the mother of invention." What does this saying mean, and what does it have to do with Benjamin Franklin?

READ
THINK
EXPLAIN

_____

_____

_____

_____

_____

_____

8 Think about Franklin's inventions and the services he established. How did these help the people of the American colonies?

READ
THINK
EXPLAIN

_____

_____

_____

_____

_____

_____

_____

STOP

Name _____   Date _____

Generalize

Directions Read the paragraph below. Then use the information to complete the graphic organizer. Generalize about the Florida Constitution.

Each state in the United States has its own constitution. The Florida Constitution is divided into 12 articles. The first article is the Florida Declaration of Rights, which resembles the United States Bill of Rights. Articles 3, 4, and 5 of the Florida Constitution outline the state government. Like the national government, the Florida state government is divided into three branches—legislative, executive, and judicial. The governor of Florida heads the executive branch. The legislative branch has a Senate and a House of Representatives. The judicial branch includes the Florida Supreme Court, the highest court in the state.

REMEMBER:
* **When you generalize, you summarize a group of facts and show the relationships between them.**

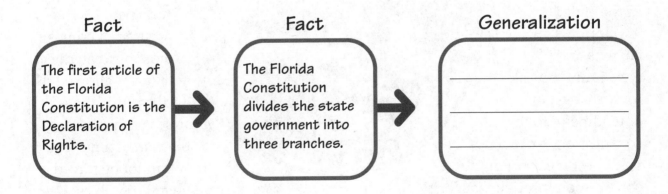

Fact
> The first article of the Florida Constitution is the Declaration of Rights.

Fact
> The Florida Constitution divides the state government into three branches.

Generalization
> _____
> _____
> _____

LA.A.2.2.1(5.1) extends previously learned knowledge and skills of the fourth grade with increasingly complex reading texts and assignments and tasks (for example, explicit and implicit ideas).
LA.A.2.2.5(5.1) reads and organizes information from multiple sources for a variety of purposes (for example, supporting opinions, predictions, and conclusions; writing a research report; conducting interviews; taking a test; performing tasks).

Lesson 1: Approving the Constitution

⭐ **Focus Skill**

Building Text Comprehension
Generalize

Directions Read the passage below. Then use the information from the passage to complete the graphic organizer on the next page. Base your generalizations on what you have read.

Over the course of 130 years, the people of Florida changed their constitution six times. They adopted the present constitution in 1968. The Florida Constitution is the plan of government for the state. It sets up the state's local and state governments, voting laws, taxes, and school system. The Florida Constitution also protects the rights of the people in the state.

Florida's citizens and legislature can ask for a change, or amendment, to the constitution. An amendment becomes part of the constitution through a majority vote by the people of Florida.

Article I of the Florida Constitution is called the Declaration of Rights. The Declaration of Rights closely resembles the United States Bill of Rights. It gives the people of Florida rights that the government cannot change. The Declaration of Rights is divided into 25 sections. The first 8 sections protect the people's basic rights. Basic rights include the freedom of speech, the freedom to practice a religion, and the freedom to gather in groups.

Beginning with section 9, the Declaration of Rights outlines how people accused of crimes must be treated. They are allowed a trial by jury, they cannot be tried twice for the same crime, and they cannot be forced to testify against themselves.

The final three sections of the Declaration of Rights protect people's privacy, allow people to look at public documents, and discuss the rights of taxpayers.

(continued)

© Harcourt

LA.A.2.2.1(5.1) extends previously learned knowledge and skills of the fourth grade with increasingly complex reading texts and assignments and tasks (for example, explicit and implicit ideas).
LA.E.2.2.4(5.2) identifies the major information in a nonfiction text.

Name _____ Date _____

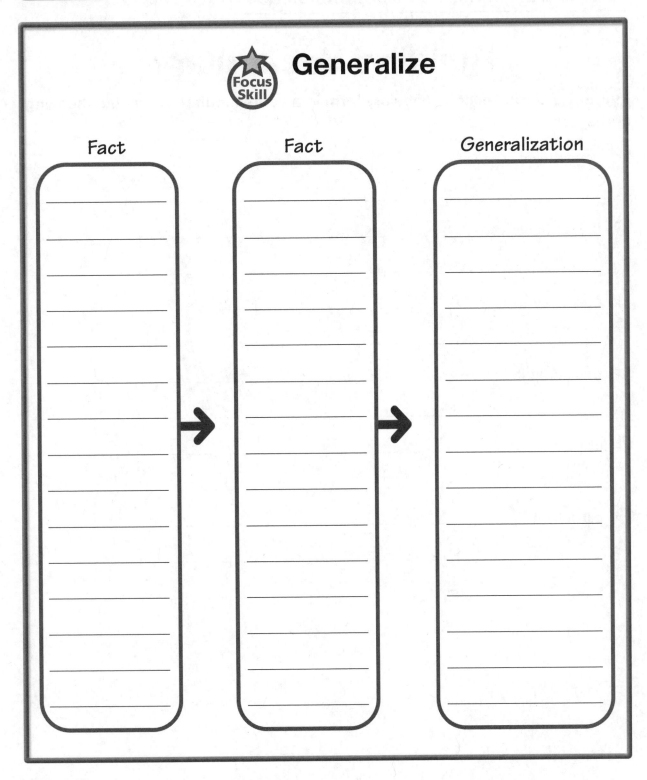

Generalize
Focus Skill

| Fact | Fact | Generalization |

LA.A.2.2.1(5.1) extends previously learned knowledge and skills of fourth grade level with increasingly complex reading texts and assignments and tasks (for example, explicit and implicit ideas).
LA.A.2.2.5(5.1) reads and organizes information from multiple sources for a variety of purposes (for example, supporting opinions, predictions, and conclusions; writing a research report; conducting interviews; taking a test; performing tasks).

87   **Reading Support for Social Studies**

Lesson 2: Rights and Responsibilities

Building Vocabulary

Directions Use each vocabulary term in a sentence that shows the meaning of that term.

1 amendment _____

_____

2 Bill of Rights _____

_____

3 due process of law _____

_____

4 human rights _____

_____

5 jury _____

_____

6 patriotism _____

_____

LA.A.1.2.3(5.1) uses a variety of strategies to determine meaning and increase vocabulary (for example, homonyms, homophones, prefixes, suffixes, word-origins, multiple meanings, antonyms, synonyms, word relationships).
LA.A.2.2.1(5.1) extends previously learned knowledge and skills of the fourth grade level with increasingly complex reading texts and assignments and tasks (for example, explicit and implicit ideas).

Name _____ Date _____

Lesson 3: Putting the New Government to Work

Building Fluency

Directions Part A. Practice reading the terms aloud.

Vocabulary		Additional Terms	
Cabinet political party	campaign	Federalist party Democratic- Republican party	District of Columbia White House

Directions Part B. First, practice reading aloud the phrases. Then, practice reading aloud the sentences.

1 George Washington chose his Cabinet / to help him / with government issues.

2 A political party / takes a side / regarding a certain issue.

3 The Federalist party believed / in a strong national government.

4 The Democratic-Republican party / favored the rights of states.

5 The District of Columbia / was taken / from land / in Maryland and Virginia.

6 The Presidential campaign / between John Adams and Thomas Jefferson / was brutal.

Directions Part C. Turn to page 325 in your Student Edition. Read aloud the first 2 paragraphs three times. Try to improve your reading each time. Record your best time on the lines below.

Number of words	98
My best time	___
Words per minute	___

© Harcourt

LA.A.1.2.4(5.1) uses a variety of strategies to monitor reading in fifth-grade or higher level texts (for example, adjusting reading rate according to purpose and text difficulty, rereading, self-correcting, summarizing, checking other sources, class and group discussions, trying an alternate word).

FCAT

FCAT Test Prep

Directions Read the passage "Voting in 2004" before answering Numbers 1 through 7.

Voting in 2004

On Tuesday, November 2, 2004, the American people voted for the President of the United States. Voter turnout was historically high for Election Day 2004. In the 2000 election, when the Supreme Court determined that the Democratic candidate had lost the vote in Florida by about 500 votes, the American people took notice. For the first time in decades, many realized the importance of their votes.

George W. Bush

Months before Election Day 2004, volunteers from the Republican Party, the Democratic Party, and other non-profit organizations hit the streets to register people to vote. One of the main groups targeted by the volunteers was young people, from ages 18 to about 25.

Traditionally, many young people do not vote because they think that their vote does not count. In 2004, however, that opinion changed. Celebrities traveled across the United States to speak to young people about the importance of voting. They reminded young people that, as American citizens, the right to vote is a valued responsibility.

The campaigns to encourage people to vote were highly successful. About 10 million new voters registered in 2004, and about 15 million more people voted than did in the 2000 election. The voter turnout rate had not been that high since 1968!

One voter, Leroy Chiao of Galveston County, Texas, made voting history. He became the first American to vote for President from space. Chiao is an astronaut living at the international space station. Chiao, whose family is originally from China, sees voting as a privilege. His vote from space was intended to show others that every vote counts.

Back on Earth, voter turnout was so high in some cities that people stood in line for hours to vote. Voters learned early the next morning that Republican George W. Bush had defeated Democrat John Kerry. Although the vote was very close in some states, there was a clear winner. The American people had reelected George W. Bush for his second term as President of the United States.

Go On ▶

© Harcourt

Directions Now answer Numbers 1 through 7. Base your answers on the passage "Voting in 2004."

1 What is the main idea of the first paragraph?
- Ⓐ In 2004 many Americans realized that their votes were important.
- Ⓑ The Presidential race of 2000 was close.
- Ⓒ In 2004 Americans voted for their President.
- Ⓓ Tuesday, November 2, 2004 was Election Day.

2 One of the main groups targeted by volunteers registering people to vote was
- Ⓕ senior citizens.
- Ⓖ working mothers.
- Ⓗ young people.
- Ⓘ recent immigrants.

3 About how many new voters registered to vote in 2004?
- Ⓐ 3 million
- Ⓑ 4 million
- Ⓒ 10,000
- Ⓓ 10 million

4 Which of the following statements is NOT true?
- Ⓕ Leroy Chiao is the first American to vote for President from space.
- Ⓖ More people voted for President in 2004 than in 2000.
- Ⓗ George W. Bush and John Kerry ran for President in 2004.
- Ⓘ Voting on Election Day 2004 went swiftly with no long lines.

5 The campaigns to register people to vote were
- Ⓐ highly successful.
- Ⓑ poorly run.
- Ⓒ not very important.
- Ⓓ only run by the Republican party.

6 The word *nonprofit* in the second paragraph means
- Ⓕ used to make money.
- Ⓖ highly educated.
- Ⓗ not used to make money.
- Ⓘ political.

Go On ▶

7 Write a paragraph describing voter turnout on Election Day 2004.

READ
THINK
EXPLAIN

_____

_____

_____

_____

_____

_____

_____

_____

_____

_____

_____

_____

_____

_____

_____

_____

_____

_____

_____

_____

_____

STOP

Name _____ Date _____

 **Draw Conclusions**

Directions **Read the paragraph below. Then use the information to complete the graphic organizer.**

At the end of the Revolutionary War, Florida was returned to Spain. In 1784 the governor of East Florida, Vincent Manuel Zespedes (SAYS•pay•days), offered land grants to anyone willing to settle in East Florida. Florida became home to British, Spanish, and American people. Thomas Jefferson and other leaders of the United States were happy about the land grants and about the number of Americans who accepted them.

REMEMBER:
- **When you draw conclusions, you combine new facts with facts you already know to make a general statement about an idea or event.**

Facts I Know

Spain owned Florida after the Revolutionary War.

New Facts

Conclusion

LA.A.2.2.5(5.1) reads and organizes information from multiple sources for a variety of purposes (for example, supporting opinions, predictions, and conclusions; writing a research report; conducting interviews; taking a test; performing tasks).
LA.E.1.2.2(5.3) makes inferences and draws conclusions regarding story elements of a fifth grade or higher level text (for example, the traits, actions, and motives of characters; plot development; setting).
LA.E.2.2.4(5.2) identifies the major information in a nonfiction text.

Name _____ Date _____

Lesson 1: Across the Appalachians

Building Text Comprehension
Draw Conclusions

Directions Read the passage below. Then use the information from the passage to complete the graphic organizer on the next page.

About ten years before Daniel Boone cleared a road through the Cumberland Gap, he explored the Florida wilderness. In the spring of 1765, several of Boone's friends arrived at his home in North Carolina. They invited Boone on an adventure to the south.

Much of Florida was wilderness area. Britain wanted people to move to Florida and build settlements. The British government offered free land to people who moved there.

Boone enjoyed exploring, and he wanted more land, so he agreed to lead an expedition to Florida. He promised his wife, Rebecca, that he would be home for Christmas dinner. Christmas was about nine months away.

With Boone on the journey were his brother, Squire, and his friends John Stewart, John Field, and William Hill. They traveled about 500 miles (about 800 km) before they reached the northern edge of Florida. Once in Florida, several of the explorers were disappointed. The heat, swamps, and insects made travel

Daniel Boone

difficult. In addition, they could not find enough wildlife to hunt for food. Boone, however, liked Florida. He enjoyed being on a frontier, where there were few people. He decided to claim land on the Gulf Coast near Pensacola.

Boone kept his promise and returned home on Christmas Day. He had many exciting stories to tell his family. He described plants, trees, and animals that he had never seen before. He told Rebecca that they were moving to Florida, but Rebecca did not want to go. She wanted to stay near her family in North Carolina. In the end, Rebecca won, and the Boones did not move south.

(continued)

LA.A.2.2.5(5.1) reads and organizes information from multiple sources for a variety of purposes (for example, supporting opinions, predictions, and conclusions; writing a research report; conducting interviews; taking a test; performing tasks).
LA.E.1.2.2(5.3) makes inferences and draws conclusions regarding story elements of a fifth grade or higher level text (for example, the traits, actions, and motives of characters; plot development; setting).
LA.E.2.2.4(5.2) identifies the major information in a nonfiction text.

Name _____ Date _____

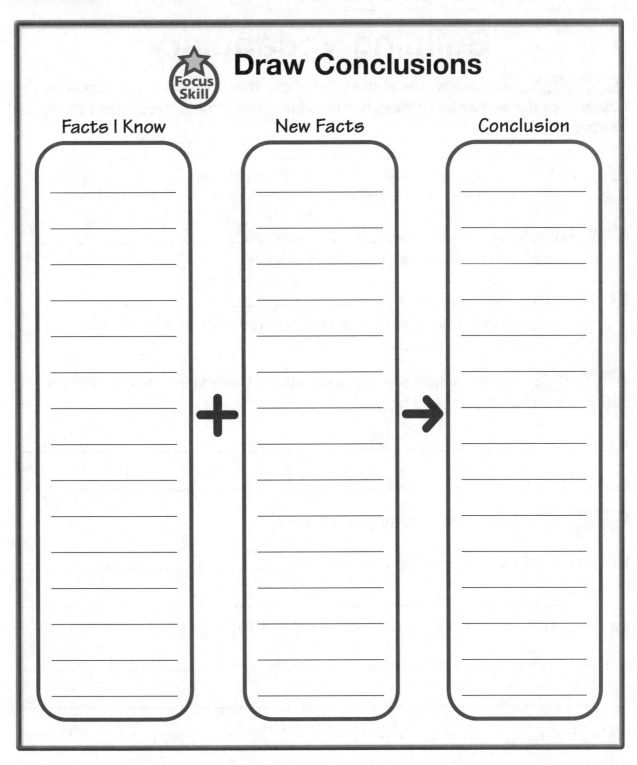

Draw Conclusions

Focus Skill

| Facts I Know | New Facts | Conclusion |

LA.A.2.2.5(5.1) reads and organizes information from multiple sources for a variety of purposes (for example, supporting opinions, predictions, and conclusions; writing a research report; conducting interviews; taking a test; performing tasks).
LA.E.1.2.2(5.3) makes inferences and draws conclusions regarding story elements of a fifth grade or higher level text (for example, the traits, actions, and motives of characters; plot development; setting).

© Harcourt

Name _____ Date _____

Building Vocabulary

Directions Read the words in the Word Box. Then complete the sentences below. Use the sentence context to help you choose the correct word for each sentence.

purchase	pathfinder

1 President Jefferson asked Meriwether Lewis to be a _____ on an expedition to learn about an unknown region.

2 The United States agreed to buy, or _____, the land reaching from the Mississippi River west to the Rocky Mountains and from New Orleans north to Canada.

Directions Define each of the following words. Use the information from the sentences above if you need help.

3 purchase: _____

4 pathfinder: _____

Directions Answer the following questions.

5 Why did the United States *purchase* new land? _____

_____

6 What kinds of hardships do you think *pathfinders* had to live through during the

early 1800s? Were there any rewards for their bravery? _____

_____

_____

A.1.2.3(5.1) uses a variety of strategies to determine meaning and increase vocabulary (for example, ͻnyms, homophones, prefixes, suffixes, word-origins, multiple meanings, antonyms, synonyms, word ͻnships).

ᒷ.2.1(5.1) extends previously learned knowledge and skills of the fourth grade level with increasingly complex texts and assignments and tasks (for example, explicit and implicit ideas).

Name _____ Date _____

Reading Biographies

Directions Read the passage about Dolley Madison. Then answer the questions.

Dolley Madison
Character Trait: Kindness

Dolley Madison was born Dolley Payne in 1768, in North Carolina. At the age of 22, she married her first husband, John Todd. In the fall of 1793, her husband and their youngest son died from yellow fever.

About a year later, Dolley Madison became friends with James Madison. Soon after, the two were married. James Madison served as the secretary of state under Thomas Jefferson. President Jefferson was widowed, so Dolley Madison greeted guests at the White House.

When James Madison became President, Dolley Madison's reputation as a good hostess grew. Once a week, she opened the White House to the public. She also visited the homes of every new member of Congress.

In 1814 British troops invaded Washington, D.C. Before escaping, Dolley Madison gathered valuable items, including a portrait of George Washington, from the White House and sent them to the Bank of Maryland for safekeeping. Her actions set an example for future First Ladies—to be both kind and brave.

1 How might other First Ladies follow Dolley Madison's example?

_____

_____

2 How did Dolley Madison demonstrate **kindness**? _____

_____

_____

LA.E.1.2.1(5.3) reads a variety of literary and informational texts (for example, fiction, drama, poetry, myths, fantasies, historical fiction, biographies, autobiographies, textbooks, manuals, magazines).
LA.E.1.2.2(5.3) makes inferences and draws conclusions regarding story elements of a fifth grade or higher level text (for example, the traits, actions, and motives of characters; plot development; setting).

Lesson 4: *By the Dawn's Early Light: The Story of "The Star-Spangled Banner"*

Building Fluency

Directions Part A. Practice reading the terms aloud.

Vocabulary	
Francis Scott Key	Anacreon
Fort McHenry	cartel boat
ramparts	stanzas
powder magazine	

Directions **Part B. First, practice reading aloud the phrases. Then, practice reading aloud the sentences.**

1 The ramparts refer / to the protective barriers / that Francis Scott Key and the others saw / around Baltimore.

2 Major George Armistead / prepared for battle / by placing sandbags / around the powder magazine.

3 Key wrote the "The Star-Spangled Banner" / to the tune / of the song "To Anacreon in Heaven."

4 The cartel boat / was finally returned / to Key and his friends.

5 After Key / and his friends had rested / in Baltimore, / he finished the four stanzas / of his poem.

6 The first title / of "The Star-Spangled Banner" / was "The Defense of Fort McHenry."

Directions **Part C. Turn to page 365 in your Student Edition. Read aloud the first paragraph three times. Try to improve your reading each time. Record your best time on the lines below.**

Number of words	**101**
My best time	_____
Words per minute	_____

© Harcourt

LA.A.1.2.4(5.1) uses a variety of strategies to monitor reading in fifth-grade or higher level texts (for example, adjusting reading rate according to purpose and text difficulty, rereading, self-correcting, summarizing, checking other sources, class and group discussions, trying an alternate word).

FCAT Test Prep

Directions Read the passage "The Louisiana Purchase" before answering Numbers 1 through 7.

The Louisiana Purchase

The Louisiana Purchase doubled the size of the United States. But just how did the United States acquire all this land? Sieur de La Salle claimed the Louisiana region in 1682 for the French. Then in 1762 it was ceded to Spain. In 1800 Spain grew tired of all the problems it was having in North America and gave Louisiana back to France. Thomas Jefferson, who was then President of the United States, was interested in purchasing only New Orleans and West Florida.

Jefferson sent James Monroe and Robert Livingston to Paris to offer to buy New Orleans and West Florida from the French. The French, however, offered to sell all of the Louisiana territory. Monroe and Livingston were not sure if they should buy the entire area without Jefferson's approval, but they decided it was too good an offer to refuse. They signed a treaty to buy the land.

Jefferson did not know if gaining land through purchase was legal. The Constitution did not say anything about this, but it did allow for treaties with other countries. So Jefferson submitted the treaty to the Senate, and it was approved.

The one problem with the treaty was that it did not state the boundaries of the Louisiana Purchase. Jefferson claimed that the purchase included the part of West Florida from Louisiana to the present-day Alabama-Florida border.

The Louisiana Purchase

Go On ▶

FCAT

Directions Now answer Numbers 1 through 7. Base your answers on the passage "The Louisiana Purchase."

1 Which country claimed Louisiana in 1682?

Ⓐ Britain

Ⓑ France

Ⓒ the United States

Ⓓ Spain

2 Which of the following statements is NOT true?

Ⓕ In 1762 Spain had control of Louisiana.

Ⓖ The treaty did not state the boundaries of the Louisiana Purchase.

Ⓗ The French offered to sell a portion of Louisiana to the United States.

Ⓘ The Constitution did not say anything about buying land.

3 Before the Louisiana region could become part of the United States, its purchase had to be approved by

Ⓐ a vote of the people.

Ⓑ the President's Cabinet.

Ⓒ the Senate.

Ⓓ Monroe and Livingston.

4 Thomas Jefferson wanted to purchase

Ⓕ all of Louisiana.

Ⓖ half of Louisiana.

Ⓗ all of Louisiana except New Orleans.

Ⓘ only New Orleans and West Florida.

5 In this passage, the word *treaty* means

Ⓐ a terrible argument.

Ⓑ an agreement between countries.

Ⓒ a misunderstanding between two people.

Ⓓ a large area of land.

6 How did the United States acquire the Louisiana Purchase?

Ⓕ France sold the land to the United States.

Ⓖ The United States claimed Louisiana.

Ⓗ The United States tricked Spain.

Ⓘ France gave away the land for free.

© Harcourt

Go On ▶

FCAT

7 Thomas Jefferson wanted to buy New Orleans and West Florida. Write a paragraph about why Monroe and Livingston hesitated to buy the entire Louisiana territory without Jefferson's approval.

READ
THINK
EXPLAIN

_____

_____

_____

_____

_____

_____

_____

_____

_____

_____

_____

_____

_____

_____

_____

© Harcourt

Name _____ Date _____

Sequence

Directions Read the paragraph below. Then use the information to complete the graphic organizer.

Before the Industrial Revolution, people made cloth by hand. The Industrial Revolution sped up the process by introducing large machines to do most of the work. The first step of turning cotton or wool into cloth is cleaning. Machines remove dirt, insects, seeds, and twigs from the fiber. The clean fiber is then carded, or combed, and spun into yarn. The final step is to turn the yarn into cloth. Workers place the yarn on a large machine called a loom. The loom weaves the yarn into a solid piece of cloth.

REMEMBER:
* A sequence is the order in which events occur.
* Words such as *first, then, next, before, after,* and *later* show sequence.

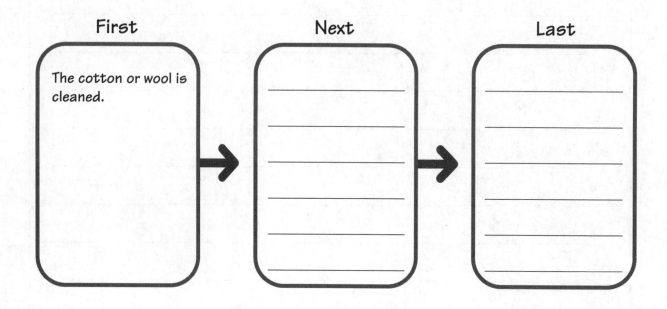

LA.A.2.2.1(5.1) extends previously learned knowledge and skills of the fourth grade level with increasingly complex reading texts and assignments and tasks (for example, explicit and implicit ideas).
LA.E.2.2.4(5.2) identifies the major information in a nonfiction text.

Lesson 1: The Industrial Revolution

⭐ Focus Skill Building Text Comprehension
Sequence

Directions Read the passage below. Then use the information from the passage to complete the graphic organizer on the next page. Identify the sequence of events.

In the mid-1800s many New England girls went to work in textile mills. Most were girls who had made about fifty cents a week cooking and cleaning for the wealthy. The textile mills paid about $14 a month.

Mill girls stayed in boardinghouses next door to the factory. About 30 girls lived in each boardinghouse. Four to six girls shared a room, with two to three girls to a bed.

Each day started at 4:30 A.M., with the ringing of the factory bells. The girls had twenty minutes to dress and rush to the factory. Work started promptly at 5:00 A.M. A clerk stood at the gate, keeping track of late arrivals.

Each girl had a job. The older, skilled girls ran the weaving looms, watching over three to four looms at once. The factory rooms were hot and dusty. Most windows were nailed shut because a breeze could break the thread.

At 7:00 A.M. the mill girls had their first break. They hurried to the boardinghouse to eat breakfast and rushed to be back at work by 7:45 A.M. When the bells rang again at noon for dinner, the girls had

thirty minutes to eat and return to work. That was their last break of the day.

The girls worked steadily until a quitting bell rang at 7:00 P.M. Once back at the boardinghouse, they had an evening meal. Exhausted, many went straight to bed. Others stayed up to study, write, or sew. The final bell of the day rang at 10:00 P.M. At that time the boardinghouse doors were locked and candles were snuffed for the night.

(continued)

LA.A.2.2.1(5.1) extends previously learned knowledge and skills of the fourth grade level with increasingly complex reading texts and assignments and tasks (for example, explicit and implicit ideas).
LA.E.2.2.4(5.2) identifies the major information in a nonfiction text.

© Harcourt

Name _____ Date _____

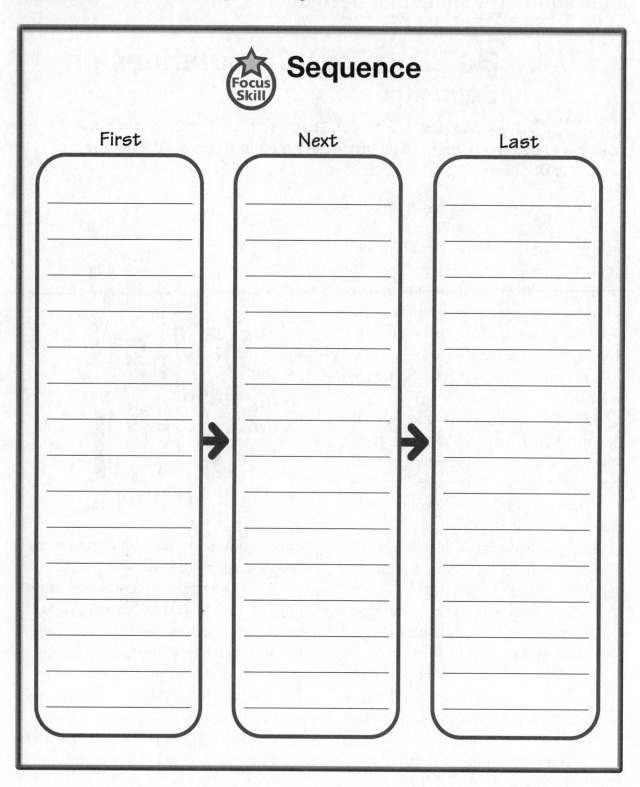

Sequence
Focus Skill

First   Next   Last

LA.A.2.2.1(5.1) extends previously learned knowledge and skills of the fourth grade level with increasingly complex reading texts and assignments and tasks (for example, explicit and implicit ideas).
LA.E.2.2.4(5.2) identifies the major information in a nonfiction text.

© Harcourt

Lesson 2: The Age of Jackson

Building Fluency

Directions **Part A. Practice reading the terms aloud.**

Vocabulary		Additional Terms	
sectionalism	secede	Liberty Bell	Indian Removal Act
states' rights	ruling	Old Hickory	Trail of Tears
		preserved	

Directions **Part B. First, practice reading aloud the phrases. Then, practice reading aloud the sentences.**

1 The Liberty Bell / tolled in honor / of John Adams and Thomas Jefferson / when they died.

2 President Andrew Jackson / earned the nickname Old Hickory, / because he was / an extremely tough man.

3 Many states / practiced regional loyalty, / called sectionalism.

4 Jackson and his Vice President, John C. Calhoun, / disagreed on the issue / of states' rights.

5 Jackson believed / that the Union should be preserved.

6 South Carolina threatened / to secede when Congress / passed another tariff in 1832.

7 Congress passed the Indian Removal Act / in 1830, / which forced the Native Americans / to leave the East.

8 In 1832 / Jackson ignored the Supreme Court's ruling / that protected the Cherokees / and their land in Georgia.

9 The long, painful journey / traveled by the Indians / from east to west / became known as the Trail of Tears.

Directions **Part C. Turn to page 379 in your Student Edition. Read aloud the first paragraph three times. Try to improve your reading each time. Record your best time on the lines below.**

Number of words	**106**
My best time	_____
Words per minute	_____

LA.A.1.2.4(5.1) uses a variety of strategies to monitor reading in fifth-grade or higher level texts (for example, adjusting reading rate according to purpose and text difficulty, rereading, self-correcting, summarizing, checking other sources, class and group discussions, trying an alternate word).

Name _____ Date _____

Reading Biographies

Directions Read the passage about David Levy Yulee. Then use what you have learned to answer the questions below.

David Levy Yulee
Character Trait: Responsibility

David Levy Yulee was born in the West Indies in 1810. When he was about 11 years old, his father, Moses, bought more than 50,000 acres of land near Jacksonville. There he built a plantation called New Pilgrimage to serve as a colony for Jews who were living in north-central Florida. Like his father, David had a sense of responsibility, a vision, and a dream, and it all involved the growth of Florida.

David Levy Yulee went to law school in St. Augustine and then entered politics. He first served as a territorial representative in the United States Congress. Because he felt it was his responsibility to help guide Florida's growth, he was an outspoken supporter for Florida's statehood. Yulee argued that making Florida a state would provide it with money for railroads and ports. This would help Florida's economy, since parts of Florida had no way to transport goods over water.

Florida became a state in 1845, and shortly after that David Levy Yulee became the first Jew ever to be elected to the United States Senate. After leaving the Senate, Yulee helped ensure that railroad service would extend through Florida by having the first cross-state railroad built. He also added telegraph and mail routes.

The town of Yulee and the county of Levy were named to honor the father, Moses, and his son, David.

1 Why was David Levy Yulee an outspoken supporter for Florida's statehood?

_____

_____

2 How did David Levy Yulee show **responsibility** to Florida? _____

_____

_____

© Harcourt

LA.E.1.2.1(5.3) reads a variety of literary and informational texts (for example, fiction, drama, poetry, myths, fantasies, historical fiction, biographies, autobiographies, textbooks, manuals, magazines).
LA.E.1.2.2(5.3) makes inferences and draws conclusions regarding story elements of a fifth grade or higher level text (for example, the traits, actions, and motives of characters; plot development; setting).

Lesson 4: An Age of Reform

Building Vocabulary

Directions Next to each vocabulary term is a list of words. Three of the words have something in common with the vocabulary term, and one does not. Identify and circle the word that does not belong in the list. Then write one or two sentences explaining why the word does not belong.

1 reform: **A.** change   **B.** improve   **C.** decline   **D.** develop

_____

_____

2 public school: **A.** education   **B.** private   **C.** teachers   **D.** open

_____

_____

3 abolish: **A.** begin   **B.** end   **C.** stop   **D.** halt

_____

_____

4 abolitionist: **A.** slavelord   **B.** Quaker   **C.** slave   **D.** Sojourner Truth

_____

_____

5 equality: **A.** freedom   **B.** rights   **C.** liberty   **D.** slavery

_____

_____

6 suffrage: **A.** vote   **B.** representation   **C.** disassociation   **D.** participation

_____

_____

LA.A.1.2.3(5.1) uses a variety of strategies to determine meaning and increase vocabulary (for example, homonyms, homophones, prefixes, suffixes, word-origins, multiple meanings, antonyms, synonyms, word relationships).
LA.A.1.2.3(5.4) uses resources and references such as a dictionary, thesaurus, and context to build word meanings.

FCAT Test Prep

Directions Read the passage "The History of the Alamo" before answering Numbers 1 through 8.

The History of the Alamo

Long before the Alamo became the site of a historic battle, it was a mission, or church. Spanish missionaries built the church in the early 1700s in what is today San Antonio, Texas. They called it the Mission San Antonio de Valero. Over the next 300 years, the Mission San Antonio de Valero would serve as a mission, a fort, and a museum.

In the late 1700s Spain gave the Mission San Antonio de Valero to the local people. They continued to live and farm at the mission, but they no longer used it as a church.

In 1803 the Spanish once again took over the Mission San Antonio de Valero. They turned it into a barracks, or a place to house soldiers. The soldiers changed the name from *Mission San Antonio de Valero* to *the Alamo*. *Alamo* is Spanish for "cottonwood."

In 1821 Mexico declared its independence from Spain. The Alamo was now under Mexican rule. About 15 years later, Texans fought for their independence from Mexico. One of the major battles of the Texas Revolution took place at the Alamo. For 13 days Texas rebels defended the Alamo from the Mexican army. Although Texas lost the Alamo, it won the fight for independence.

Texas became a state of the United States in 1845. Soon after, the United States Army used the Alamo as a place to house troops and store supplies.

In 1905 the Texas state legislature made the Alamo a memorial to the heroes of the Texas Revolution. Today the Alamo is a museum.

Go On ▶

Directions Now answer Numbers 1 through 8. Base your answers on the passage "The History of the Alamo."

1 The Alamo has served as
- Ⓐ a school, a hospital, and a fort.
- Ⓑ a mission, a school, and a museum.
- Ⓒ a mission, a fort, and a museum.
- Ⓓ a hospital, a church, and a farm.

2 Which of the following statements is NOT true?
- Ⓕ The United States Army used the Alamo to store supplies.
- Ⓖ The Texas State Legislature made the Alamo into a memorial.
- Ⓗ Texas was once claimed by Spain.
- Ⓘ Today the Alamo is in ruins.

3 Mexico declared its independence from Spain
- Ⓐ in the early 1700s.
- Ⓑ 15 years after the Texas Revolution.
- Ⓒ in 1845.
- Ⓓ in 1821.

4 The Alamo was once known as
- Ⓕ San Antonio, Texas.
- Ⓖ the Alamo de Parras.
- Ⓗ Mission San Antonio de Valero.
- Ⓘ Cottonwood.

5 In this passage, the word *barracks* means
- Ⓐ a place to house soldiers.
- Ⓑ a historical monument.
- Ⓒ a scene of an important battle.
- Ⓓ a place where missionaries live.

6 Why did the author write the passage "The History of the Alamo"?
- Ⓕ to describe the details of the Texas Revolution
- Ⓖ to explain why Mexico wanted its independence from Spain
- Ⓗ to explain why the Alamo is a historic building
- Ⓘ to talk about early churches in Texas

Go On ▶

Name _____ Date _____

7 Explain why the Alamo is an important part of United States history.

READ
THINK
EXPLAIN

_____

_____

_____

_____

_____

_____

8 List the uses of the Alamo, from the past to present day.

READ
THINK
EXPLAIN

_____

_____

_____

_____

_____

_____

STOP

Name _____ Date _____

Directions **Read the paragraph below. Then use the information to complete the graphic organizer about Florida's economy.**

Farming was important to Florida's economy in the 1850s. Cotton was a major crop for many Florida farmers. Some farmers grew cotton on large plantations. Many of the owners of these plantations relied on a large number of enslaved Africans to work in the cotton fields. These workers were not paid for their labor and lived under a strict set of rules. Other farmers owned small farms. Many of them owned a few slaves and worked alongside them in the fields. Still others owned no slaves at all.

REMEMBER:
• **To categorize is to classify information by category. You can group people, places, and events in categories to make it easier to find facts.**

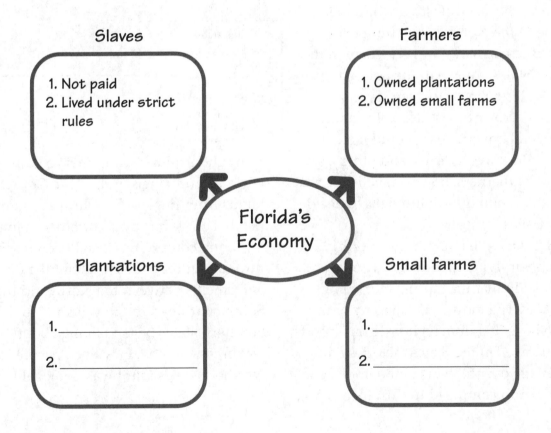

Slaves
1. Not paid
2. Lived under strict rules

Farmers
1. Owned plantations
2. Owned small farms

Florida's Economy

Plantations
1. _____
2. _____

Small farms
1. _____
2. _____

© Harcourt

LA.A.2.2.1(5.1) extends previously learned knowledge and skills of the fourth grade level with increasingly complex reading texts and assignments and tasks (for example, explicit and implicit ideas).
LA.E.2.2.4(5.2) identifies the major information in a nonfiction text.

Lesson 1: Differences Divide North and South

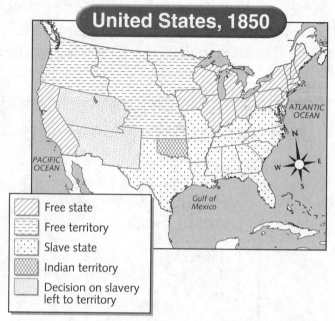

⭐ Focus Skill Building Text Comprehension
Categorize

Directions Read the passage below about conflicts between the North and the South. Then use the information from the passage to complete the graphic organizer on the next page.

During the first half of the 1800s, the differences between the North and the South caused many disagreements. These disagreements—about slavery, states' rights, the economy, and secession—were dividing the country.

Slavery had divided the country since the Constitution was written. As the country grew, the issue of slavery did, too. People in the North, or the free states, wanted to end slavery everywhere in the United States. People in the South, the slave states, wanted to keep slavery.

Many Northerners also believed that the federal government should make the laws about slavery, taxes, and other issues. Many Southerners, however, believed that each state should have the right to decide these issues for itself.

Many people living in the North made their living in industry. They were involved in manufacturing and selling products. The industrial economy of the North benefited from high taxes on imports, which gave United States factories an advantage over foreign competitors. People in the South continued to earn their living

United States, 1850

(map legend:)
- ▨ Free state
- ▦ Free territory
- ⠿ Slave state
- ▩ Indian territory
- ▨ Decision on slavery left to territory

through farming. Southerners sold their crops to Europeans and, in turn, purchased goods from Europe. The farm economy depended on slavery and low taxes on imports.

Many compromises had been reached throughout the mid-1800s, but the disagreements between the North and the South continued to grow. People in Southern states began talking about leaving the Union. However, people in Northern states felt it was not legal to leave the Union.

(continued)

LA.A.2.2.1(5.1) extends previously learned knowledge and skills of the fourth grade level with increasingly complex reading texts and assignments and tasks (for example, explicit and implicit ideas).
LA.E.2.2.4(5.2) identifies the major information in a nonfiction text.

Directions Complete the graphic organizer.

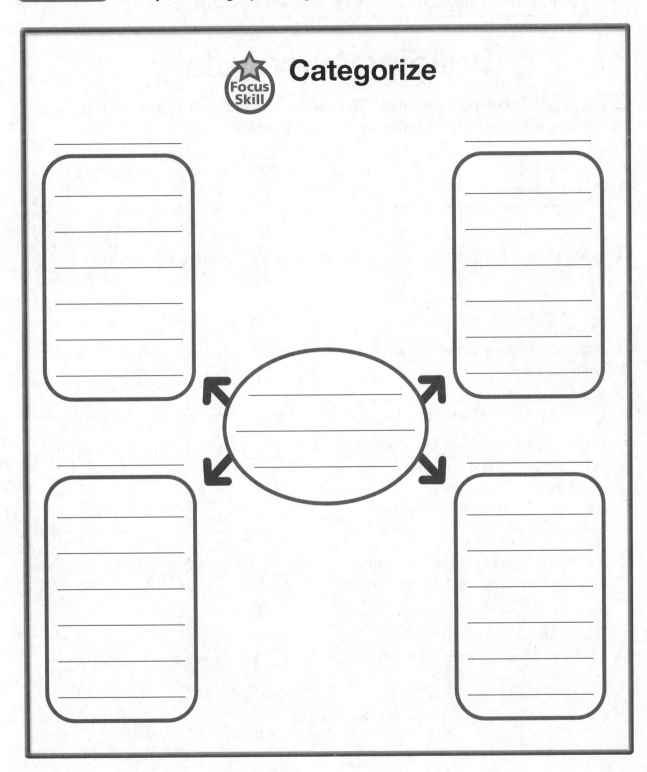

⭐ Categorize
Focus Skill

LA.A.2.2.1(5.1) extends previously learned knowledge and skills of the fourth grade level with increasingly complex reading texts and assignments and tasks (for example, explicit and implicit ideas).
LA.E.2.2.4(5.2) identifies the major information in a nonfiction text.

Lesson 2: Africans in Slavery and Freedom

Building Vocabulary

Directions Read each sentence. Then write on the line the term from the box that means the same as the underlined word or words.

slave code	spirituals	Underground Railroad
overseer	resist	

1 Some slaves chose to <u>act against</u> slavery by leading rebellions against white slave owners.

_____

2 The <u>supervisor</u> watched the slaves closely to see if any were falling behind in their work.

_____

3 Because of the <u>group of laws that shaped the day-to-day lives of enslaved people</u>, a woman could not leave her owners' land to visit her sister on the neighboring plantation.

_____

4 Harriet Tubman relied on the <u>system of escape routes leading to freedom</u> to guide hundreds of escaped slaves to free states in the North.

_____

5 Many enslaved people expressed their feelings about slavery by singing <u>religious songs based on Bible stories</u>.

_____

LA.A.1.2.3(5.1) uses a variety of strategies to determine meaning and increase vocabulary (for example, homonyms, homophones, prefixes, suffixes, word-origins, multiple meanings, antonyms, synonyms, word relationships).
LA.A.2.2.1(5.1) extends previously learned knowledge and skills of the fourth grade level with increasingly complex reading texts and assignments and tasks (for example, explicit and implicit ideas).

Lesson 3: Facing a National Problem

Building Fluency

Directions Part A. Practice reading the terms aloud.

Vocabulary	Additional Terms	
free states slave states	Missouri Compromise Compromise of 1850 Fugitive Slave Law Kansas-Nebraska Act	Bleeding Kansas Dred Scott Republican party

Directions Part B. First, practice reading aloud the phrases. Then, practice reading aloud the sentences.

1 The Missouri Compromise / was designed by Henry Clay / to keep the peace / between free states and slave states.

2 The Compromise of 1850 / contained the Fugitive Slave Law, / which said anyone caught helping slaves to escape / would be punished.

3 Kansas became / the center of attention / after the Kansas-Nebraska Act was passed.

4 The dispute over slavery / that killed more than 200 people / was known as Bleeding Kansas.

5 The Dred Scott decision / did not settle / the battle / over slavery.

6 Abraham Lincoln was a part / of the Republican party, / a party that was formed / to fight the spread of slavery.

Directions Part C. Turn to page 429 in your Student Edition. Read aloud the first 2 paragraphs under "The Lincoln-Douglas Debates" three times. Try to improve your reading each time. Record your best time on the lines below.

Number of words	108
My best time	____
Words per minute	____

© Harcourt

LA.A.1.2.4(5.1) uses a variety of strategies to monitor reading in fifth-grade or higher level texts (for example, adjusting reading rate according to purpose and text difficulty, rereading, self-correcting, summarizing, checking other sources, class and group discussions, trying an alternate word).

Lesson 4: A Time for Hard Decisions

Reading Biographies

Directions Read the passage about Madison Starke Perry. Then use what you have learned to answer the questions on the next page.

Madison Starke Perry
Character Trait: Citizenship

Madison Starke Perry was born in South Carolina in 1814. In 1845 he moved to Alachua County, Florida, where he ran a plantation and made a name for himself as an orator. In 1849 Perry showed the importance of citizenship by becoming a member of the Florida House of Representatives. In 1850 he was elected to the Florida Senate. Then, in 1857, Perry became Florida's fourth governor.

During his time in office, Perry accomplished many things. First, he was able to oversee the expansion and completion of the Florida railroad. Next, he was responsible for several new counties joining Florida. Then, he helped settle a dispute with Georgia over the Florida-Georgia boundary. Finally, because he thought there was a chance that Florida would join the South in seceding from the Union, he reestablished the state militia.

Perry was in favor of secession. He said, "The only hope the Southern states have for domestic peace . . . is dependent on their action now; and that proper action is—Secession. . . . " Just as Perry

anticipated, Florida did secede from the Union in 1861. Men were ready to fight for the Confederate army.

At the end of his term as governor, Perry continued his dedication to Florida and once again showed good citizenship by becoming a colonel in the Seventh Infantry Regiment. He served in this regiment until 1863, when he was forced to retire due to illness. Madison Stark Perry died in 1865 in Rochelle, Florida. He was 51 years old.

(continued)

LA.E.1.2.1(5.3) reads a variety of literary and informational texts (for example, fiction, drama, poetry, myths, fantasies, historical fiction, biographies, autobiographies, textbooks, manuals, magazines).

Name _____ Date _____

1 What did Perry accomplish during his term as governor of Florida?

_____

_____

_____

2 What is the meaning of the word *orator* in the first paragraph?

_____

_____

_____

3 Judging by Perry's quote, why do you think he was in favor of Florida's seceding from the Union?

_____

_____

_____

CHARACTER EDUCATION How did Madison Starke Perry demonstrate **citizenship**?

_____

_____

_____

© Harcourt

LA.E.1.2.1(5.3) reads a variety of literary and informational texts (for example, fiction, drama, poetry, myths, fantasies, historical fiction, biographies, autobiographies, textbooks, manuals, magazines).
LA.E.1.2.2(5.3) makes inferences and draws conclusions regarding story elements of a fifth grade or higher level text (for example, the traits, actions, and motives of characters; plot development; setting).

Use with Chapter 13, Lesson 4. **117** **Reading Support for Social Studies**

FCAT Test Prep

Directions Read the passage "Statehood for Florida" before answering Numbers 1 through 7.

Statehood for Florida

By the late 1830s more than 48,000 people lived in the Florida Territory. Since a population of 60,000 was needed to become a state, many Floridians began to talk about the advantages and disadvantages of joining the United States.

Many East Floridians felt it would be better to wait until the population was large enough to form two states. Then there would be more Southern states in the United States, so the South would have more power in Congress than the North. Another reason people in East Florida did not want to become a state was because it would cost money. Once Florida was no longer a territory, the people of the state would have the responsibility of paying taxes for government services.

David Levy Yulee, a territorial representative in Congress, argued that Florida should become one state. There would be more money for improvements in the state. Some settlers in Middle Florida felt this way, too. They also wanted to choose their own leaders and wanted representation in Congress, including voting rights.

One group of people living in West Florida wanted West Florida to join Alabama. Another agreed that Florida

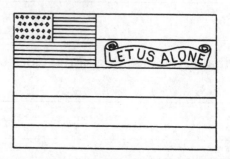

should be one state. The only point on which everyone agreed was that they all wanted representation and votes in Congress.

Finally, in 1838, white men over 21 years old voted for statehood. A year later, in 1839, Florida submitted its constitution to the United States Congress for approval.

Congress had even more difficulty approving statehood for Florida than Florida's settlers had applying for it. The reason was Florida's wish to be admitted as a slave state. If this happened, there would be more slave states than free states in the United States.

After six years of debate, Congress reached an agreement. If Iowa joined the United States as a free state, then Florida could join as a slave state. The number of free and slave states would remain equal. Florida accepted the compromise, and in 1845 it became the twenty-seventh state to join the United States.

Go On ▶

© Harcourt

Directions Now answer Numbers 1 through 7. Base your answers on the passage "Statehood for Florida."

1 Which statement is the BEST summary for this passage?

Ⓐ People in Florida wanted to choose their own leaders.

Ⓑ It took a long time for Florida to apply for statehood.

Ⓒ There were many disagreements within Florida and Congress about statehood for Florida.

Ⓓ Congress had to approve Florida's constitution before it could become a state.

2 What did many people living in East Florida want to do about statehood?

Ⓕ They wanted to wait until the population was large enough to form two states.

Ⓖ They wanted to remain a territory and not become a state.

Ⓗ They wanted to make Florida one state.

Ⓘ They wanted Florida to become part of Alabama.

3 Why were most people who lived in Middle Florida and West Florida in favor of statehood?

Ⓐ They wanted to pay taxes.

Ⓑ They wanted representation and votes in Congress.

Ⓒ They wanted East Florida to be its own state.

Ⓓ They did not want railroads and new ports to be built.

4 Why did it take so long for Congress to approve statehood for Florida?

Ⓕ Florida wanted to be admitted as a free state.

Ⓖ Florida's constitution stated slaves could not be freed.

Ⓗ Florida wanted more representation in Congress.

Ⓘ Florida wanted to be admitted as a slave state.

5 To give up some of what you want in order to reach an agreement is a

Ⓐ compromise.

Ⓑ debate.

Ⓒ vote.

Ⓓ declaration.

6 In what year did Florida become a state?

Ⓕ 1838

Ⓖ 1839

Ⓗ 1845

Ⓘ 1846

Go On ▶

© Harcourt

Name _____ Date _____

7 Write a paragraph in which you explain why you think it was important to Congress that the number of free states and slave states remained equal.

READ
THINK
EXPLAIN

_____

_____

_____

_____

_____

_____

_____

_____

_____

_____

_____

_____

_____

_____

_____

_____

© Harcourt

Name _____ Date _____

# Summarize

Directions Read the paragraph below. Then use the information to complete the graphic organizer. Summarize facts about the Gettysburg Address.

On November 19, 1863, President Abraham Lincoln went to Gettysburg, Pennsylvania, to dedicate a cemetery in memory of the soldiers who had died there. He gave a short speech that day. The speech, later known as the Gettysburg Address, was no longer than three minutes. Lincoln spoke about the ideals of liberty and equality. He honored the fallen soldiers, and he urged Americans to try to win the struggle that the men died for so that the Union would be preserved. Although the speech was short, it was an inspiring one.

REMEMBER:
- **When you summarize, you tell a shortened version of what you have just read.**

Facts

1. On November 19, 1863, President Abraham Lincoln delivered the Gettysburg Address.
2. Lincoln spoke about the ideals of liberty and equality.
3. Lincoln honored the fallen soldiers.
4. Lincoln urged Americans to try to preserve the Union.

Summary

_____

_____

_____

_____

_____

_____

© Harcourt

LA.A.2.2.5(5.1) reads and organizes information from multiple sources for a variety of purposes (for example, supporting opinions, predictions, and conclusions; writing a research report; conducting interviews; taking a test; performing tasks).
LA.E.2.2.4(5.2) identifies the major information in a nonfiction text.

Name _____   Date _____

 **Building Text Comprehension**
Summarize

Directions Read the passage below about Florida life during the Civil War. Then use the information from the passage to complete the graphic organizer on the next page.

During the Civil War, life was not only hard for the Confederate and Union soldiers, but it was also hard for people not fighting in the war. In Florida, women and older men took over the farms, plantations, and businesses that were deserted by young men who went to fight.

Shortages of food, medicine, and weapons were felt throughout Florida. People experienced shortages because of the blockades, or barriers. The Union set up these blockades along the Florida coast to stop trade between Britain and the Confederate states. Floridians learned to survive with very little.

Most Floridians helped each other. A group called the Ladies' Military Aid helped with the shortages by making blankets, uniforms, and shoes for soldiers. Mary Martha Reid, the widow of a former governor of the Florida Territory, helped start a hospital in Richmond, Virginia, for Florida soldiers. While she was there, Reid improved ways of healing the wounded soldiers. Her inventiveness greatly reduced the number of deaths in that particular hospital.

Florida surrendered to the Union army on April 26, 1865. To enforce their victory,

Union troops rode through Florida and told the slaves they were free. In order to be allowed back into the Union, Florida had to abolish slavery, write a new constitution, and swear its loyalty to the United States. Florida also had to give all adult males the right to vote and approve the Fourteenth Amendment. This amendment said that everyone who is born in the United States is a citizen. Many Southern states did not agree with the amendment. However, Florida did what the Union asked and, in 1868, became a state once again. Florida did all these things, and Floridians were soon able to return to their lives.

Mary Martha Reid

(continued)

LA.A.2.2.1(5.1) extends previously learned knowledge and skills of the fourth grade level with increasingly complex reading texts and assignments and tasks (for example, explicit and implicit ideas).
LA.E.2.2.4(5.2) identifies the major information in a nonfiction text.

© Harcourt

Name _____ Date _____

Focus Skill

Summarize

Facts

_____
_____
_____
_____
_____
_____
_____
_____
_____
_____
_____
_____
_____
_____
_____

→

Summary

_____
_____
_____
_____
_____
_____
_____
_____
_____
_____
_____
_____
_____
_____
_____

LA.A.1.2.4(5.1) uses a variety of strategies to monitor reading in fifth-grade or higher level texts (for example, adjusting reading rate according to purpose and text difficulty, rereading, self-correcting, summarizing, checking other sources, class and group discussions, trying an alternate word).
LA.A.2.2.1(5.1) extends previously learned knowledge and skills of the fourth grade level with increasingly complex reading texts and assignments and tasks (for example, explicit and implicit ideas).
LA.E.2.2.4(5.2) identifies the major information in a nonfiction text.

Lesson 2: *The Signature That Changed America*

Building Fluency

Directions Part A. Practice reading the terms aloud.

Vocabulary	
Emancipation Proclamation	convictions
hesitated	sentiment
resolution	

Directions Part B. First, practice reading aloud the phrases. Then, practice reading aloud the sentences.

1 Abraham Lincoln did not want people / to think / that he hesitated / in signing his proclamation.

2 As a legislator, / Lincoln signed a resolution / against slavery.

3 Lincoln's convictions / led him / to delay the unveiling / of the Emancipation Proclamation.

4 People's sentiment / concerning the proclamation / was one of bitterness and fear.

Directions Part C. Turn to page 446 in your Student Edition. Read aloud the first two paragraphs three times. Try to improve your reading each time. Record your best time on the lines below.

Number of words	107
My best time	_____
Words per minute	_____

© Harcourt

LA.A.1.2.4(5.1) uses a variety of strategies to monitor reading in fifth-grade or higher level texts (for example, adjusting reading rate according to purpose and text difficulty, rereading, self-correcting, summarizing, checking other sources, class and group discussions, trying an alternate word).

Lesson 3: The Long Road to a Union Victory

Building Vocabulary

Directions Each of the words below describes some things that took place in the 1860s. Write each word from the Word Box next to its definition.

> Gettysburg Address   assassination

1 Lincoln's speech that spoke of his ideals of liberty and equality on which he believed the country had been founded _____

_____

2 the murder of a political leader _____

Directions **Answer the following questions.**

3 Why were Northerners and Southerners shocked by the **assassination** of President Lincoln? _____

_____

_____

4 Why was Lincoln's **Gettysburg Address** so important? _____

_____

5 Write a paragraph on what the **Gettysburg Address** means to you.

_____

_____

_____

_____

_____

LA.A.1.2.2(5.1) refines previously learned knowledge and skills of the fourth grade with increasingly complex reading selections and assignments and tasks (for example, decoding, context clues, predicting, variety of word structure, constructing meaning, purposes of reading).

© Harcourt

Lesson 4: Life After the War

Reading Biographies

Directions Read the passage about Jonathan C. Gibbs. Then use what you have learned to answer the questions on the next page.

Jonathan C. Gibbs
Character Trait: Responsibility

Jonathan C. Gibbs was born in Philadelphia, Pennsylvania, in 1827. Both his parents were free African Americans. As a young adult, Gibbs graduated from Dartmouth College and then attended Princeton Theological Seminary. When the Civil War ended, Gibbs started a private school in North Carolina for freed slaves. Then, in 1867, he went to Florida, also to teach former slaves. Since he had been born free, he had learned to read and write. He felt that it was his responsibility to give freed slaves the same opportunities he had.

In 1868 Gibbs was appointed secretary of state, the first African American to serve in this position. He was secretary of state for four years. Then he was appointed superintendent of public instruction. That meant that he was in charge of all public schools in Florida.

As superintendent of public instruction, Gibbs worked to make public schools in Florida better. He wanted the 200,000 or so Floridians who could not read or write to receive an education. Gibbs created a system for choosing standard textbooks

for schools. He also made sure that there were schools for African Americans. Gibbs was responsible for the introduction of a bill in the state legislature that established what is known today as Florida A&M University.

Jonathan Gibbs was not well liked by members of the Ku Klux Klan because he was an African American in a responsible position. It is believed that for safety he often slept in the attic of his house. He died in 1874. Some people believed that he was poisoned, but that was never proved. A high school in St. Petersburg is named for him.

(continued)

LA.E.1.2.1(5.3) reads a variety of literary and informational texts (for example, fiction, drama, poetry, myths, fantasies, historical fiction, biographies, autobiographies, textbooks, manuals, magazines).
LA.E.2.2.4(5.2) identifies the major information in a nonfiction text.

© Harcourt

Name _____ Date _____

Directions Read the time line about Jonathan C. Gibbs. Then answer the questions below using the time line and the biography on page 126.

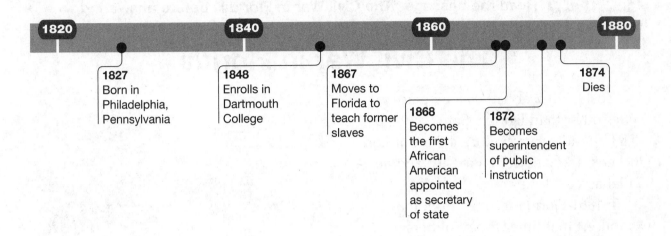

1 In what year did Gibbs become superintendent of public instruction? _____

2 Did Gibbs move to Florida or enroll in Dartmouth first? _____

_____

3 When did Gibbs become the first African American appointed as secretary of state?

_____

How did Jonathan C. Gibbs demonstrate **responsibility**?

_____

_____

_____

_____

_____

_____

LA.E.1.2.1(5.3) reads a variety of literary and informational texts (for example, fiction, drama, poetry, myths, fantasies, historical fiction, biographies, autobiographies, textbooks, manuals, magazines).
LA.E.1.2.2(5.3) makes inferences and draws conclusions regarding story elements of a fifth grade or higher level text (for example, the traits, actions, and motives of characters; plot development; setting).
LA.E.2.2.4(5.2) identifies the major information in a nonfiction text.

FCAT Test Prep

Directions Read the passage "The Civil War in Florida" before answering Numbers 1 through 8.

The Civil War in Florida

Most Civil War battles took place in states other than Florida. Some of the battles that did occur in Florida were at Fort Pickens, Tampa, near Lake City, and near Tallahassee.

In 1861 Florida seceded from the Union. At that time Union soldiers were stationed at Fort Pickens near Pensacola. Confederate soldiers tried to force Union soldiers to give up Fort Pickens. When the Union soldiers refused, Confederate troops attacked a Union camp outside the fort. The fighting continued until May 1862, when Confederate troops were forced out of the area. The Union occupied Pensacola until the end of the war.

Then in June of the same year, Union soldiers entered the Tampa area and called for the Confederate militia to surrender. The militia stationed there, the Osceola Rangers, refused to give up even when the Union general attacked. Within two days, the Union soldiers stopped firing and left the area because they realized the Osceola Rangers were determined not to lose Tampa.

In 1864, near Lake City, the largest Civil War battle in Florida, the Battle of Olustee (oh•LUHS•tee), took place. Under the command of General Truman A. Seymour, 5,500 Union troops entered Lake City. General Seymour was planning to destroy food supplies being grown there.

Battle of Olustee

Confederate General Joseph Finegan organized 5,200 Confederate soldiers to block the Union army. The battle was over after about six hours, and the Confederate troops were victorious.

In 1865 another large battle, the Battle of Natural Bridge, occurred near Tallahassee. Union Major General John Newton had his soldiers march northeast to Tallahassee. When a Confederate militia group spotted them, the militia burned a bridge so the Union soldiers would be unable to get across the St. Marks River. Both groups met at Natural Bridge, a place where the river goes underground. The Confederate soldiers were able to keep the Union soldiers from controlling the area. Tallahassee became the only Confederate state capital east of the Mississippi River not to be seized by the Union.

Go On ▶

Directions Now answer Numbers 1 through 8. Base your answers on the passage "The Civil War in Florida."

1 Which city in Florida did the Union army occupy until the Civil War ended?

Ⓐ Lake City

Ⓑ Pensacola

Ⓒ Tallahassee

Ⓓ Fort Pickens

2 Which event happened SECOND?

Ⓕ fighting at Fort Pickens

Ⓖ the Battle of Natural Bridge

Ⓗ the Battle of Olustee

Ⓘ fighting at Tampa

3 The largest Civil War battle in Florida was

Ⓐ the battle at Fort Pickens.

Ⓑ the Battle of Natural Bridge.

Ⓒ the Battle of Olustee.

Ⓓ the battle at Tampa.

4 With victory at the Battle of Olustee, the Confederate army was able to prevent the Union army from

Ⓕ destroying food supplies.

Ⓖ controlling all of Florida.

Ⓗ blocking Confederate troops.

Ⓘ traveling on the St. Marks River.

5 The Battle of Olustee was important to Florida because

Ⓐ the Union army was victorious.

Ⓑ the Confederate army was victorious.

Ⓒ about 11,000 soldiers fought in the battle.

Ⓓ it lasted six hours.

6 The Battle of Natural Bridge was an important victory for the Confederacy because

Ⓕ Tallahassee, the state capital, was now under Union control.

Ⓖ no Union ships were able to travel on Florida's rivers.

Ⓗ Tallahassee, the state capital, remained under Confederate control.

Ⓘ no lives were lost.

Go On ▶

© Harcourt

Name _____ Date _____

7 The Confederate soldiers defeated the Union soldiers at Natural Bridge. Explain why this was important to Florida and to the Confederacy.

READ
THINK
EXPLAIN

_____

_____

_____

_____

_____

_____

_____

_____

_____

8 Few battles were fought in Florida during the Civil War. Why do you think this was so?

READ
THINK
EXPLAIN

_____

_____

_____

_____

_____

_____

_____

_____

_____

STOP

Name _____ Date _____

Fact and Opinion

Directions **Read the paragraph below. Then use the information to complete the graphic organizer about growth in Florida.**

Up until the 1880s, Florida's economy relied on plantations that grew cotton, tobacco, and other crops. Then in 1883 a business owner named Henry B. Plant began building a railroad along Florida's west coast. Plant's railroad connected Florida to the northern states. Along the railroad line, Plant built the state's finest and most luxurious hotels, which attracted visitors from the north. Many of the visitors decided to live in Florida permanently because of the state's beautiful beaches and comfortable climate. As more people moved into Florida, the state grew, which gave rise to new industries and jobs.

REMEMBER:

- **A fact is a statement that can be proved to be true.**

- **An opinion is an individual's view of something, shaped by that person's feelings.**

Florida's Population and Reasons for Its Growth

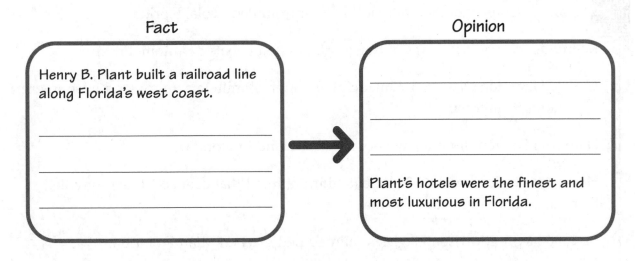

Fact

Henry B. Plant built a railroad line along Florida's west coast.

_____

_____

_____

Opinion

_____

_____

_____

Plant's hotels were the finest and most luxurious in Florida.

LA.A.2.2.6(5.1) extends the expectations of the fourth grade with increasingly complex reading selections, assignments and tasks (for example, differences between fact, fiction, opinion).
LA.E.2.2.4(5.2) identifies the major information in a nonfiction text.

Lesson 1: Big Business and Industrial Cities

⭐ **Focus Skill** # Building Text Comprehension
Fact and Opinion

Directions Read the statements below about Florida. Decide whether each statement is a fact or an opinion. Write the number of each one in the correct column of the graphic organizer on the next page.

1 The Industrial Revolution occurred more slowly in Florida than in other states.

2 In the 1800s Florida's farmers grew sugarcane, cotton, corn, tobacco, and vegetables.

3 In 1880 more than 260,000 people lived in Florida.

4 Everyone who lived in Florida in 1880 led an exciting, fast-paced life.

5 Henry B. Plant built hotels and steamship lines.

6 Henry B. Plant's railroad became known as the Atlantic Coast Line Railroad.

7 Without railroads, Florida would not have grown.

8 William D. Chipley built a railroad line east from Pensacola, Florida.

9 Railroads are a better means of transportation than boats or automobiles.

10 In 1881 Hamilton Disston of Philadelphia bought 4 million acres of land in southern Florida for $1 million.

11 Hamilton Disston did not pay very much for land in Florida.

12 Henry M. Flagler bought a 36-mile (58-km) railroad that connected Jacksonville, Florida, and St. Augustine, Florida.

13 By 1896 Henry Morrison Flagler's railroad had reached Miami, Florida.

14 Henry Morrison Flagler was Florida's most important businessperson.

(continued)

LA.A.2.2.6(5.1) extends the expectations of the fourth grade with increasingly complex reading selections, assignments and tasks (for example, differences between fact, fiction, opinion).
LA.E.2.2.4(5.2) identifies the major information in a nonfiction text.

© Harcourt

Name _____ Date _____

★ Focus Skill **Fact and Opinion**

Fact

Opinion

→

LA.A.2.2.6(5.1) extends the expectations of the fourth grade with increasingly complex reading selections, assignments and tasks (for example, differences between fact, fiction, opinion).
LA.E.2.2.4(5.2) identifies the major information in a nonfiction text.

Lesson 2: Growing Pains

Building Vocabulary

Directions In each group, circle the word or words that are synonyms for, or have a similar meaning to, the vocabulary word in boldfaced type.

1 **strike**	stop work	employ	work
2 **regulate**	control	manage	lose control
3 **human resource**	unemployed person	worker	money
4 **federation**	loners	related groups	organization
5 **labor union**	concerned workers	new workers	unconcerned workers

Directions Now circle the word or words that are antonyms, or opposites, of the vocabulary words in boldfaced type

6 **strike**	withhold work	employ	work
7 **regulate**	control	manage	lose control
8 **human resource**	unemployed person	worker	money
9 **federation**	loners	related groups	organization
10 **labor union**	group of workers	new workers	unconcerned workers

LA.A.2.2.1(5.1) extends previously learned knowledge and skills of the fourth grade level with increasingly complex reading texts and assignments and tasks (for example, explicit and implicit ideas).

© Harcourt

Name _____ Date _____

Reading Biographies

Directions Read the passage about Rosemary Barkett. Then use the information to answer the questions below.

Rosemary Barkett
Character Trait: Respect

Rosemary Barkett was born in Ciudad Victoria, Mexico, in 1939. In 1946 she and her family settled in Miami, Florida.

Barkett attended Spring Hill College in Alabama. In 1970 she received a law degree from the University of Florida. She practiced civil and trial law in West Palm Beach.

In 1979 Barkett became a circuit judge for the Fifteenth Judicial Circuit. Because of her outstanding record, she was appointed in 1984 to Florida's Fourth District Court of Appeals. One year later Barkett was appointed to serve as a justice on the Florida Supreme Court, the highest court in Florida. She was Florida's first female Supreme Court justice, and in 1992 she became the first female chief justice of that court. Her record on working for fairness for all individuals and protecting individual rights gave her national recognition.

Barkett has volunteered her time to serve on committees that deal with child welfare, family law, and women in law. She received the Judicial Achievement Award in 1986. She was also inducted into the Florida Women's Hall of Fame. An award has even been named after her. The Rosemary Barkett Award is presented each year to a "person who has demonstrated outstanding commitment to equal justice under the law."

1 Why was it significant that Barkett was appointed to the Florida Supreme Court?

_____

2 How is Rosemary Barkett an example of the character trait **respect**?

_____

LA.E.1.2.1(5.3) reads a variety of literary and informational texts (for example, fiction, drama, poetry, myths, fantasies, historical fiction, biographies, autobiographies, textbooks, manuals, magazines).
LA.E.1.2.2(5.3) makes inferences and draws conclusions regarding story elements of a fifth grade or higher level text (for example, the traits, actions, and motives of characters; plot development; setting).
LA.E.2.2.4(5.2) identifies the major information in a nonfiction text.

Lesson 4: *The Great Migration: An American Story*

Building Fluency

Directions Part A. Practice reading the terms aloud.

Vocabulary	
shortage	migrants
recruits	barren
ravaged	disdain
boll weevils	

Directions Part B. First, practice reading aloud the phrases. Then, practice reading aloud the sentences.

1 The factories / in the North / had a shortage of workers, / because many had left their jobs / to fight in World War I.

2 Many recruits / filled the northbound trains / in search of better lives.

3 The South's crops had been ravaged / by floods and boll weevils.

4 To African Americans, / the South was barren, / not only because crops were spoiling, / but also because their lives were in danger there.

5 African Americans who already had lived / in the North for quite some time / treated the migrants / with disdain.

Directions Part C. Turn to page 501 in your Student Edition. Read aloud the first 4 paragraphs three times. Try to improve your reading each time. Record your best time on the lines below.

Number of words	99
My best time	____
Words per minute	____

LA.A.1.2.4(5.1) uses a variety of strategies to monitor reading in fifth-grade or higher level texts (for example, adjusting reading rate according to purpose and text difficulty, rereading, self-correcting, summarizing, checking other sources, class and group discussions, trying an alternate word).

Lesson 5: The Growth of Cities

Reading Charts and Graphs

Directions Use the table to answer the questions below.

Ten Largest Cities in Florida, 2000	
City	Population
Jacksonville	736,000
Miami	362,000
Tampa	303,000
St. Petersburg	248,000
Hialeah	226,000
Orlando	186,000
Fort Lauderdale	152,000
Tallahassee	151,000
Hollywood	139,000
Pembroke Pines	137,000

1 Which cities have populations of at least 300,000?

_____

2 Which city has a smaller population, Hialeah or Hollywood?

_____

3 How many more people live in Orlando than in Tallahassee?

_____

4 How many of the cities have populations of fewer than 200,000?

_____

5 Which city has the larger population, Miami or Fort Lauderdale? What is the difference in the populations of these two cities?

_____

_____

LA.A.2.2.8(5.1) extends previously learned knowledge and skills of the fourth grade with increasingly complex texts and assignments and tasks (for example, using reference materials and processes).

© Harcourt

FCAT Test Prep

Directions Read the passage "The Growth of Florida" before answering Numbers 1 through 7.

The Growth of Florida

Three men who helped Florida grow during the late 1800s were Henry B. Plant, William D. Chipley, and Henry M. Flagler.

Henry B. Plant had a dream that trains would connect cities all over Florida. In 1885 work was completed on his South Florida Railroad. This railroad started in Sanford and went to Tampa. He added railroads that connected Kissimmee, Lakeland, and other central Florida towns. Later that year, the town of Cork, which was east of Tampa, was renamed Plant City to honor Henry B. Plant. Plant continued his railroad development, and by the early 1900s, Plant's railroad was known as the Atlantic Coast Line Railroad.

Plant also contributed to Florida's growth by building hotels. His famous Tampa Bay Hotel welcomed visitors from all over the country and the world. It was a quarter-mile-long building and had 500 rooms, all with electric lights.

William D. Chipley also built railroads. He began building railroads in 1881 that would link Florida's Panhandle with the rest of Florida. His railroad ran from Pensacola to the Apalachicola River and then connected with railroads heading to Georgia and eastern Florida. In that way, goods could be transported from the Panhandle to Pensacola.

Henry M. Flagler arrived in Florida in

William D. Chipley

Henry B. Plant   **Henry M. Flagler**

1883 and within two years started building a hotel in St. Augustine. This was the Ponce de León Hotel, and it was one of the fanciest hotels in the world. Flagler did not stop with hotel building, however. He bought the Jacksonville, St. Augustine, and Halifax River Railroad and expanded it so passengers could ride trains from New York City to St. Augustine and Daytona Beach. By 1894 Florida's East Coast Railroad carried goods, local passengers, and tourists through Florida as far as Palm Beach.

By 1900 more than 3,000 miles (4,828 km) of railroad crossed Florida. Railroads also connected Florida to other places in the United States. Henry B. Plant, William D. Chipley, and Henry M. Flagler had made that possible.

Go On ▶

© Harcourt

Directions Now answer Numbers 1 through 7. Base your answers on the passage "The Growth of Florida."

1 What is the BEST summary for this passage?

Ⓐ Henry M. Flagler built hotels and railroads near St. Augustine.

Ⓑ Henry B. Plant, William D. Chipley, and Henry M. Flagler built railroads that connected cities in Florida.

Ⓒ Henry B. Plant, William D. Chipley, and Henry M. Flagler contributed to the growth of Florida during the late 1800s.

Ⓓ By 1900 there were more than 3,000 miles of railroad in Florida.

2 Who developed railroads and hotels on Florida's east coast?

Ⓕ Henry B. Plant

Ⓖ Henry M. Flagler

Ⓗ William D. Chipley

Ⓘ all of the above

3 Which event happened FIRST?

Ⓐ The South Florida Railroad was completed.

Ⓑ William D. Chipley began building a railroad to connect the Panhandle with the rest of Florida.

Ⓒ Henry M. Flagler arrived in St. Augustine.

Ⓓ The Tampa Bay Hotel was built.

4 What was the town of Cork, Florida, renamed?

Ⓕ Pensacola

Ⓖ Flagler City

Ⓗ Chipley City

Ⓘ Plant City

5 What did Henry B. Plant want to do?

Ⓐ He wanted to connect cities all over Florida.

Ⓑ He wanted to connect cities all over the country.

Ⓒ He wanted to have hotels for tourists.

Ⓓ He wanted to build a hotel with electric lights.

6 Henry M. Flagler expanded his railroad so that

Ⓕ people living in the cities of Kissimmee and Lakeland would be able to take a train to Tampa.

Ⓖ passengers could ride trains from New York City to St. Augustine and Daytona Beach.

Ⓗ goods could be transported from the Panhandle to Pensacola.

Ⓘ tourists would have hotels in which to stay while visiting Florida.

Go On ▶

© Harcourt

Name _____   Date _____

7 Henry B. Plant, William D. Chipley, and Henry M. Flagler contributed to the growth of the state of Florida. Choose one of these men, and write a paragraph telling how and why he was able to do this.

READ
THINK
EXPLAIN

_____

_____

_____

_____

_____

_____

_____

_____

_____

_____

_____

_____

_____

_____

_____

© Harcourt

STOP

Focus Skill

Main Idea and Details

Directions Read the paragraph below. Then use the information to complete the graphic organizer with details about the Great Plains.

The Great Plains is a vast region of grasslands and plateaus that stretches north to south through the center of the United States and Canada. The region is bordered in the United States by the Rocky Mountains on the west and lowlands on the east. It extends as far north as the Arctic Ocean and as far south as the Rio Grande. Parts of ten states lie in the Great Plains—Colorado, Kansas, Montana, Nebraska, New Mexico, North Dakota, Oklahoma, South Dakota, Texas, and Wyoming.

REMEMBER:

• **The main idea of a paragraph or lesson is what the paragraph or lesson is mostly about. The main idea may be stated in a sentence, or it may be suggested.**

• **Details give more information about the main idea.**

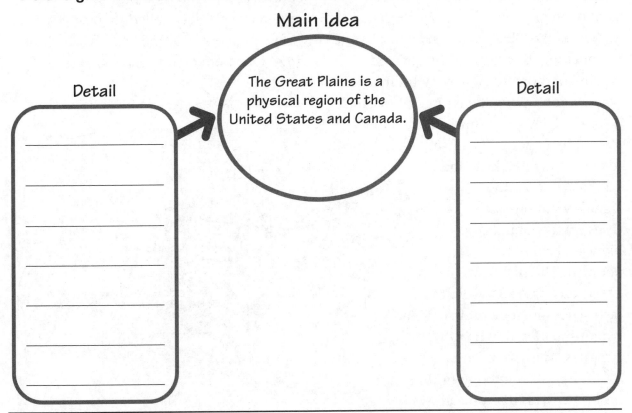

LA.A.2.2.1(5.1) extends previously learned knowledge and skills of the fourth grade level with increasingly complex reading texts and assignments and tasks (for example, explicit and implicit ideas).
LA.A.2.2.5(5.1) reads and organizes information from multiple sources for a variety of purposes (for example, supporting opinions, predictions, and conclusions; writing a research report; conducting interviews; taking a test; performing tasks).
LA.E.2.2.4(5.2) identifies the major information in a nonfiction text.

© Harcourt

Lesson 1: Farming the Great Plains

⭐ (Focus Skill) Building Text Comprehension
Main Idea and Details

Directions Read the passage below. Then use the information from the passage to complete the graphic organizer on the next page. Identify the main idea and details about the Oklahoma land rush of 1889.

On March 23, 1889, President Benjamin Harrison announced that 2 million acres of land in Indian Territory were open for settlement. Thousands of Americans were excited to hear the news. Farmers, ex-soldiers, businesspeople, families, and former slaves rushed to the borders of Indian Territory.

Under the law, settlers had to wait until noon on April 22 to enter the region, known as the Oklahoma Lands. Just before the opening, they arrived by covered wagon, on horseback, and by train at railway stations along the region's borders.

By 11:59 A.M. on April 22, each railway station had a long line of settlers waiting to rush into the Oklahoma Lands. At noon, the signals went off—rifles cracked, bugles blew, and cannons boomed. The rush was on. Those on horseback were the fastest. Others took off in covered wagons loaded down with supplies. Many hurried on foot. They all wanted to find the best plots with trees, meadows, and water.

To the settlers' surprise, many of the good lots were already claimed. Lawbreakers had slipped in earlier and illegally claimed plots. They were called "Sooners" because they entered the Oklahoma Lands too soon.

By the end of the day, close to 11,000 new homesteads dotted the Oklahoma Lands. Those who took part in the settlement proudly called themselves "Eighty-niners," for the year in which the great Oklahoma land rush took place.

(continued)

LA.A.2.2.1(5.1) extends previously learned knowledge and skills of the fourth grade with increasingly complex reading texts and assignments and tasks (for example, explicit and implicit ideas).
LA.E.2.2.4(5.2) identifies the major information in a nonfiction text.

Name _____ Date _____

Directions Complete the graphic organizer.

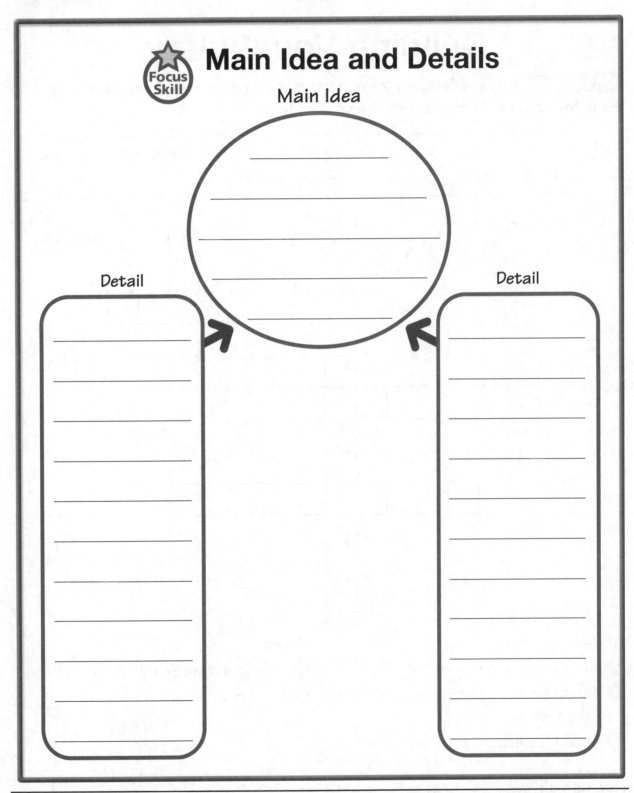

LA.A.2.2.5(5.1) reads and organizes information from multiple sources for a variety of purposes (for example, supporting opinions, predictions, and conclusions; writing a research report; conducting interviews; taking a test; performing tasks).
LA.E.2.2.4(5.2) identifies the major information in a nonfiction text.

Lesson 2: The Cattle Kingdom

Building Vocabulary

Directions Each vocabulary term in the box matches one of the clues below.
Fill in the crossword puzzle with the correct terms.

| long drive | vaqueros | range war |
| open range | barbed wire | |

Across

2 free grazing land

4 a fight between farmers and ranchers in the 1880s

5 wire with sharp points

Down

1 a long-distance cattle drive

3 the first cowhands

LA.A.1.2.3(5.1) uses a variety of strategies to determine meaning and increase vocabulary (for example, homonyms, homophones, prefixes, suffixes, word-origins, multiple meanings, antonyms, synonyms, word relationships).
LA.A.2.2.1(5.1) extends previously learned knowledge and skills of the fourth grade level with increasingly complex reading texts and assignments and tasks (for example, explicit and implicit ideas).

Lesson 3: Mining in the West

Building Fluency

Directions Part A. Practice reading the terms aloud.

Vocabulary		Additional Terms	
prospector boom	bust vigilance	Pikes Peak refineries	ghost towns mining camps

Directions Part B. First, practice reading aloud the phrases. Then, practice reading aloud the sentences.

1 In 1858 / thousands of people / came to Pikes Peak in Colorado / to search for gold.

2 A prospector usually / worked alone / to search for gold, silver, or other mineral resources.

3 As the mining towns grew, / refineries were built / to help process minerals.

4 Towns such as Denver and Boise / experienced a mining boom / when people discovered gold there.

5 People often left mining towns / during a bust, / causing them to become deserted ghost towns.

6 Many mining towns / usually started as mining camps, / where fights often started / among the miners.

7 Some communities developed Vigilance Committees / to maintain law and order.

Directions Part C. Turn to page 525 in your Student Edition. Read aloud the first paragraph three times. Try to improve your reading each time. Record your best time on the lines below.

Number of words	91
My best time	____
Words per minute	____

LA.A.1.2.4(5.1) uses a variety of strategies to monitor reading in fifth-grade or higher level texts (for example, adjusting reading rate according to purpose and text difficulty, rereading, self-correcting, summarizing, checking other sources, class and group discussions, trying an alternate word).

Lesson 4: Conflict in the West

Reading Biographies

Directions Read the passage about Chief Joseph.

Chief Joseph
Character Trait: Leadership

Chief Joseph was born in 1840 in a Nez Perce village in what is today the northeastern part of Oregon. His parents named him Hin-mah-too-yah-lat-kekht, or "Thunder Rolling Down the Mountains." He took the name Joseph as an adult.

At the time of Joseph's birth, the Nez Perce lands stretched over parts of what is today Idaho, Oregon, and Washington. The Nez Perce relied on the region's streams, rivers, and forests for food such as salmon, venison, and camas roots. Sometimes, small bands of Nez Perce crossed into Montana to hunt buffalo on the Great Plains.

Joseph grew up in a time of many changes for the Nez Perce. White settlers started moving into Nez Perce lands, bringing with them a new culture and religion. Then, in 1860, gold was discovered on Nez Perce lands. Thousands of white miners poured into the region. To avoid conflicts, the United States government ordered all Nez Perce onto a small reservation in Idaho.

By this time, Joseph had become chief of his band. He did not want a battle with the United States Army, so he agreed to move his people to the reservation. Before they could reach the reservation, however, conflicts broke out between the Nez Perce and the soldiers. Chief Joseph decided to lead his band to safety in Canada. However, the Army stopped them less than 40 miles (64 km) from the border.

Chief Joseph and his people were taken to a reservation in Indian Territory. In 1879 Chief Joseph traveled to Washington, D.C., to ask the President to let his people move home. Instead, six years later, Chief Joseph and his band were moved to the Colville Reservation in what is today Washington. Chief Joseph continued to speak out for his people's rights until his death in 1904.

© Harcourt

(continued)

LA.E.1.2.1(5.3) reads a variety of literary and informational texts (for example, fiction, drama, poetry, myths, fantasies, historical fiction, biographies, autobiographies, textbooks, manuals, magazines).
LA.E.2.2.4(5.2) identifies the major information in a nonfiction text.

Name _____   Date _____

Directions After you have read the biography on page 146, study the map below. Then use the map and the biography to answer the questions that follow.

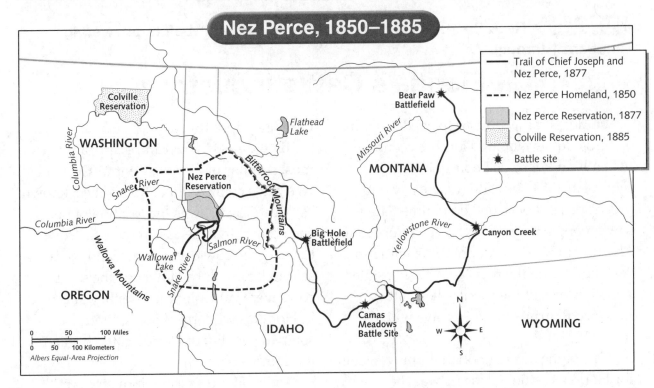

Nez Perce, 1850–1885

Legend:
— Trail of Chief Joseph and Nez Perce, 1877
--- Nez Perce Homeland, 1850
■ Nez Perce Reservation, 1877
▫ Colville Reservation, 1885
✳ Battle site

1 Compare the Nez Perce Homeland of 1850 to the Nez Perce Reservation of 1877. How do you think the change in size affected the ways of life of the Nez Perce people?

_____

_____

2 About how many miles did Chief Joseph and his band travel before being stopped by the United States Army?

_____

How is Chief Joseph an example of the character trait **leadership**?

_____

_____

LA.E.1.2.1(5.3) reads a variety of literary and informational texts (for example, fiction, drama, poetry, myths, fantasies, historical fiction, biographies, autobiographies, textbooks, manuals, magazines).
LA.E.1.2.2(5.3) makes inferences and draws conclusions regarding story elements of a fifth grade or higher level text (for example, the traits, actions, and motives of characters; plot development; setting).
LA.E.2.2.4(5.2) identifies the major information in a nonfiction text.

© Harcourt

Name _____ Date _____

FCAT Test Prep

Directions Read the passage "Florida's Cattle Industry" before answering Numbers 1 through 7.

Florida's Cattle Industry

Florida's cattle industry played a significant role in developing Florida's economy. When Juan Ponce de León arrived in Florida in 1513, the state was mostly wide, green spaces. Ponce de León immediately saw an opportunity. So when he returned to Florida in 1521, he brought cattle with him, making Florida the first cattle-raising state. No other part of the country had cattle until the Pilgrims brought cows with them in 1624.

One of the most important improvements for Florida's cattle industries was the building of railroads. This new form of transportation linked the cattle ranches to coastal ports. Using railroads took less time than hiring cowhands to guide the cattle to ports. As a result, Florida grew into one of the largest cattle-producing states east of the Mississippi River.

By the 1890s, cow camps appeared in most sections of Florida. Central Florida was cattle country. Lake Kissimmee, known as "Cow Town," was the location of one such camp. In Lake Kissimmee, the cows, called scrub cows, were small and were said to lack quality. However, the scrub cows were valuable, because they survived in Florida's wilderness areas. Pretty soon, the quality of Florida cattle began to improve.

Today Florida's cattle industry is still thriving. The state has one of the 15 largest cattle industries in the United States. East of the Mississippi, however, Florida ranks number three among the largest number of cattle in that part of the country.

© Harcourt

Go On ▶

Name _____   Date _____

Directions Now answer Numbers 1 through 7. Base your answers on the passage "Florida's Cattle Industry."

1 What year was cattle brought to Florida?
- Ⓐ 1513
- Ⓑ 1624
- Ⓒ 1501
- Ⓓ 1521

2 Which of the following statements is NOT true?
- Ⓕ Florida was the first state to raise cattle.
- Ⓖ The cattle industry is no longer one of Florida's industries.
- Ⓗ Transporting cattle on railroads took less time than hiring a cow-hand to guide the cattle.
- Ⓘ Lake Kissimmee was known as "Cow Town."

3 When Juan Ponce de León first arrived in Florida in 1513, he
- Ⓐ realized that Florida had mostly thin, brown spaces.
- Ⓑ already had cattle with him.
- Ⓒ realized that Florida had mostly wide, green spaces.
- Ⓓ decided to permanently stay in Florida.

4 In this passage, the word *cowhand* means
- Ⓕ a cow who is small and lacks quality.
- Ⓖ a person who guides the cattle to ports.
- Ⓗ the name of a town known for cattle industries.
- Ⓘ a person who builds railroads.

5 Lake Kissimmee was known as
- Ⓐ Cow City
- Ⓑ Cow Place
- Ⓒ Cow Town
- Ⓓ Cattle Town

6 Why did railroads improve the cattle industry?
- Ⓕ because they destroyed cattle ranches
- Ⓖ because they increased the value of scrub cows
- Ⓗ because they provided a fast way to get cattle to ports
- Ⓘ because they made the citrus industry go out of business

Go On ▶

© Harcourt

7 Write a paragraph that describes the development of the cattle industry in Florida.

READ
THINK
EXPLAIN

_____

_____

_____

_____

_____

_____

_____

_____

_____

_____

_____

_____

_____

_____

_____

_____

_____

_____

_____

STOP

Make Inferences

Focus Skill

Directions **Read the passage below. Then use it to complete the graphic organizer about the Panama Canal.**

When Theodore Roosevelt became President, one of his goals was to build a canal that would connect the Atlantic Ocean and the Pacific Ocean. The canal was to be built across the Isthmus of Panama. The only problem was that the isthmus did not belong to the United States. It belonged to Colombia. Colombia turned down the United States' offer of $10 million for the right to build the canal.

At the time, Colombia ruled Panama. President Roosevelt let the people of Panama know that he would support a revolution to end Colombian rule. In this way the United States would be able to build a canal across the isthmus.

After the revolution, the people of Panama created a new nation. The United States then got the right to build the canal. American ports on the Atlantic coast would now be connected to those on the Pacific coast, making it easier to ship goods.

REMEMBER:
- **When you make an inference, you use facts and your experiences to come to a conclusion about something.**

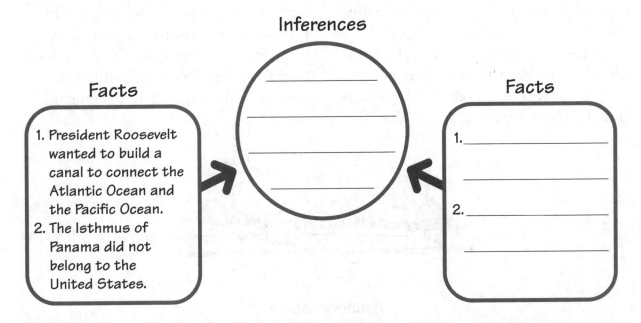

LA.A.2.2.1(5.1) extends previously learned knowledge and skills of the fourth grade level with increasingly complex reading texts and assignments and tasks (for example, explicit and implicit details).
LA.E.1.2.2(5.3) makes inferences and draws conclusions regarding story elements of a fifth grade or higher level text (for example, the traits, actions, and motives of characters; plot development; setting).
LA.E.2.2.4(5.2) identifies the major information in a nonfiction text.

Name _____ Date _____

⭐ Building Text Comprehension
Focus Skill
Make Inferences

Directions Read the passage below about the Spanish-American War. Then complete the graphic organizer on the next page.

At the end of the 1800s, Spain controlled two colonies in the Western Hemisphere—Cuba and Puerto Rico. Since Cuba is about 90 miles (145 km) from the coast of Florida, many Cubans moved to Florida at that time. Many of these Cuban immigrants wanted independence for Cuba. So did many other people living in the United States.

In 1898 President William McKinley sent the battleship *Maine* to Havana, Cuba, to protect Americans living in Cuba. Within three weeks, the *Maine* exploded and sank, killing 260 sailors. Spain was blamed for the sinking. The United States declared war on Spain in April 1898.

Since Florida is so close to Cuba, many Florida cities, such as Tampa, became military bases. Theodore Roosevelt formed the Rough Riders, a fighting group. The Tampa Bay Hotel was the headquarters for the Rough Riders and other troops stationed in Tampa.

Although the Spanish-American War lasted less than four months, more than 5,000 American soldiers died. While some died from fighting, most died from malaria and yellow fever. Clara Barton, a nurse during the Civil War, cared for many of the sick and wounded soldiers during the Spanish-American War. She was stationed in Tampa.

As a result of the Spanish-American War, the United States gained land and became a world power. Spain gave the United States control of Cuba, Puerto Rico, and other holdings. The war helped Florida as well. Florida's population grew as soldiers moved to the military bases.

Battleship *Maine*

(continued)

LA.A.2.2.1(5.1) extends previously learned knowledge and skills of the fourth grade level with increasingly complex reading texts and assignments and tasks (for example, explicit and implicit details).
LA.E.1.2.2(5.3) makes inferences and draws conclusions regarding story elements of a fifth grade or higher level text (for example, the traits, actions, and motives of characters; plot development; setting).
LA.E.2.2.4(5.2) identifies the major information in a nonfiction text.

© Harcourt

Name _____ Date _____

Directions Complete the graphic organizer.

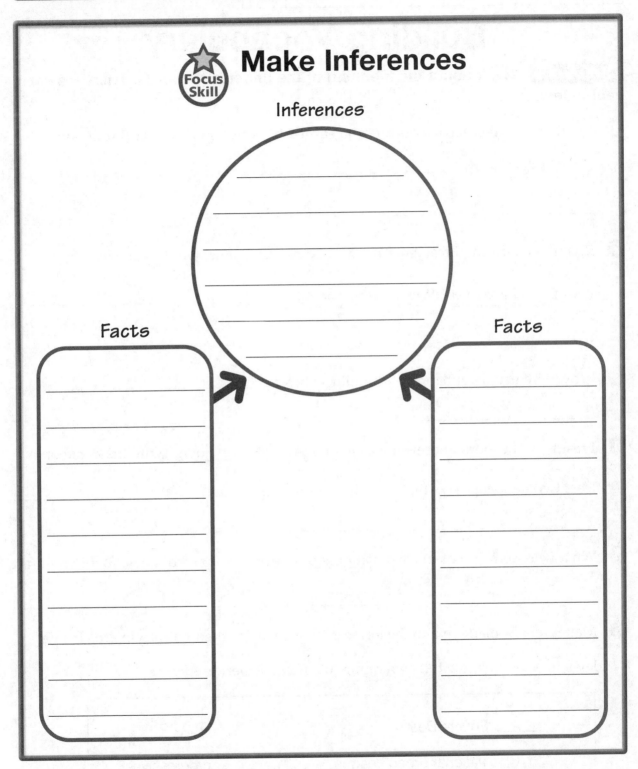

Make Inferences

Inferences

Facts

Facts

LA.A.2.2.1(5.1) extends previously learned knowledge and skills of the fourth grade level with increasingly complex reading texts and assignments and tasks (for example, explicit and implicit ideas).
LA.E.1.2.2(5.3) makes inferences and draws conclusions regarding story elements of a fifth grade or higher level text (for example, the traits, actions, and motives of characters; plot development; setting).
LA.E.2.2.4(5.2) identifies the major information in a nonfiction text.

Lesson 2: Progressives and Reform

Building Vocabulary

Directions Think about the meaning of the underlined words. Then answer each question.

1 Would you rather have a doctor who earned his job from favors or through the

merit system? Why? _____

_____

2 If you lived during President Theodore Roosevelt's time, would you have agreed

with the progressives? Why or why not? _____

_____

3 Why were people unhappy with political bosses? _____

_____

4 President Theodore Roosevelt was interested in conservation. Write the name of at

least two national parks that President Roosevelt formed. _____

_____

5 What were some problems that commissions pursued throughout the Progressive Era?

_____

6 Make a check mark next to the term specifically associated with trying to change

laws that did not give full civil rights to African Americans.

_____	Square Deal	_____	NAACP
_____	National Urban League	_____	progressives

LA.A.1.2.3(5.5) identifies, classifies, and demonstrates knowledge of levels of specificity among fifth-grade or higher level words from a variety of categories.
LA.A.2.2.1(5.1) extends previously learned knowledge and skills of the fourth grade level with increasingly complex reading texts and assignments and tasks (for example, explicit and implicit ideas).

© Harcourt

Lesson 3: The Great War

Building Fluency

Directions Part A. Practice reading the terms aloud.

Vocabulary		Additional Terms	
alliance military draft	no-man's-lands isolation	Allied Powers Central Powers U-boat	trenches dogfights

Directions Part B. First, practice reading aloud the phrases. Then, practice reading aloud the sentences.

1 The Central Powers consisted of / Germany, Austria-Hungary, / the Ottoman Empire, and Bulgaria.

2 To protect themselves, / some European countries formed an alliance.

3 A U-boat sank / the British passenger ship *Lusitania*.

4 In April 1917 / the United States joined the Allied Powers / in World War I.

5 The United States Congress / issued a military draft / during World War I.

6 Most of the fighting / in World War I took place / in the trenches of France, / which were separated by no-man's-lands.

7 The fighting also took place / in air battles called dogfights.

8 After World War I, / many Americans wanted the United States / to adopt a policy / of isolation.

Directions Part C. Turn to page 559 in your Student Edition. Read aloud the first two paragraphs three times. Try to improve your reading each time. Record your best time on the lines below.

Number of words	91
My best time	____
Words per minute	____

LA.A.1.2.4(5.1) uses a variety of strategies to monitor reading in fifth-grade or higher level texts (for example, adjusting reading rate according to purpose and text difficulty, rereading, self-correcting, summarizing, checking other sources, class and group discussions, trying an alternate word).

© Harcourt

FCAT

FCAT Test Prep

Directions Read the passage "Women, Voting, and the League of Women Voters" before answering Numbers 1 through 8.

Women, Voting, and the League of Women Voters

The Nineteenth Amendment to the United States Constitution was ratified in 1920. It gave all American women the right to vote. It had been more than 70 years since Lucretia Mott and Elizabeth Cady Stanton first organized a women's rights convention in July 1848 in Seneca Falls, New York. At that convention the attendees listed the reforms they believed were needed.

In 1890 the National American Woman Suffrage Association was formed. Carrie Lane Chapman Catt was its president. Some states had already given women the right to vote in certain elections, such as school board elections. Some states had even given women full voting rights in

state elections. Finally, in 1919, President Woodrow Wilson decided it was time to support women's suffrage. The Nineteenth Amendment was ratified one year later.

In 1920 the National American Woman Suffrage Association became the League of Women Voters. Catt wanted women voters to be informed and to become involved in politics. She wrote, "The politicians used to ask us why we wanted the vote. They seemed to think that we want to do something particular with it. . . . They did not understand that women wanted to help make the general welfare."

Today the League of Women Voters works at all levels of government to keep people informed on issues. Throughout the 1900s, the League supported such issues as civil rights, actions to clean up the environment, and affordable housing and child care. Now, the League continues to inform women and men on important issues.

Because of women like Lucretia Mott, Elizabeth Cady Stanton, and Carrie Lane Chapman Catt, women today not only vote but also serve in public offices at all levels of government.

Carrie Lane Chapman Catt

© Harcourt

Go On ▶

Directions Now answer Numbers 1 through 8. Base your answers on the passage "Women, Voting, and the League of Women Voters."

1 What does *women's suffrage* refer to?

Ⓐ women's right to receive equal pay

Ⓑ rights guaranteed by the Constitution

Ⓒ women's right to vote

Ⓓ special government boards

2 Before the Nineteenth Amendment was passed,

Ⓕ all states allowed women to vote in state elections.

Ⓖ some states allowed women to vote in state elections.

Ⓗ some states allowed women to vote in national elections.

Ⓘ no states allowed women to vote.

3 Who was responsible for the formation of the League of Women Voters?

Ⓐ Lucretia Mott

Ⓑ Susan B. Anthony

Ⓒ Elizabeth Cady Stanton

Ⓓ Carrie Lane Chapman Catt

4 Why was the ratification of the Nineteenth Amendment important?

Ⓕ It gave all American women the right to vote in all elections.

Ⓖ It gave all Americans the right to vote.

Ⓗ It gave women the right to run for public office.

Ⓘ It led to reforms in civil rights.

5 Which is NOT a major goal of the League of Women Voters?

Ⓐ electing a woman as President of the United States

Ⓑ supporting environmental issues

Ⓒ working for affordable child care

Ⓓ informing people on issues

6 Because of Lucretia Mott, Elizabeth Cady Stanton, and Carrie Lane Chapman Catt, women today

Ⓕ have equal educational opportunities.

Ⓖ have more free time.

Ⓗ hold public offices at all levels of government.

Ⓘ are informed on all important government issues.

Go On ▶

FCAT

7 Carrie Lane Chapman Catt said that politicians "did not understand that women wanted to help make the general welfare." What do you think she meant by "the general welfare"? Why do you think she worked so hard for women's suffrage?

READ
THINK
EXPLAIN

_____

_____

_____

_____

_____

8 Today, how does the League of Women Voters fulfill Carrie Lane Chapman Catt's vision?

READ
THINK
EXPLAIN

_____

_____

_____

_____

_____

_____

_____

_____

STOP

© Harcourt

Name _____   Date _____

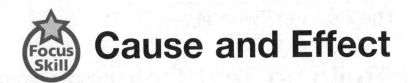

Cause and Effect

Directions Read the passage below. Then use it to complete the graphic organizer about the rise of dictators in Europe after World War I.

After World War I, economies and political systems in some European countries were unstable. Dictators were able to rise to power in some countries very quickly. In Germany Adolf Hitler said that Germany had been unfairly treated after World War I. People had little money and less hope, and they listened to his promises that Germany would once again become a powerful nation. Hitler formed a political party called the National Socialists, or Nazis. Nazi soldiers destroyed or imprisoned all who disagreed with them. In 1933 the Nazis took control of Germany, and Hitler became its ruler.

Other dictators were Benito Mussolini (buh•NEE•toh moo•suh•LEE•nee) in Italy, Francisco Franco in Spain, Joseph Stalin in the Soviet Union, and Hirohito (hir•oh•HEE•toh) in Japan. Other nations, including the United States and Britain, did little to stop the rise of those dictatorships. Some of the dictators began to invade other countries.

REMEMBER:

• **A cause is an event or action that makes something else happen.**

• **An effect is what happens as a result of that event or action.**

Rise of Dictators After World War I

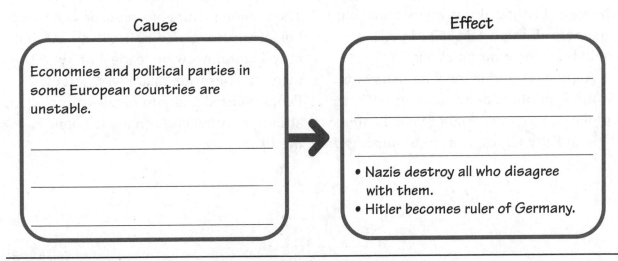

Cause

Economies and political parties in some European countries are unstable.

_____

_____

_____

Effect

_____

_____

_____

• Nazis destroy all who disagree with them.
• Hitler becomes ruler of Germany.

LA.A.2.2.1(5.1) extends previously learned knowledge and skills of the fourth grade level with increasingly complex reading texts and assignments and tasks (for example, explicit and implicit ideas).
LA.E.2.2.1(5.1) understands cause-and-effect relationships in literary texts.
LA.E.2.2.4(5.2) identifies the major information in a nonfiction text.

Lesson 1: The Roaring Twenties

Building Text Comprehension
Cause and Effect

Directions Read the passage below about America's boom economy. Then use the information from the passage to complete the graphic organizer on the next page.

When World War I ended, the factories that had made war supplies started to make new products. New industries started to produce wanted goods. Americans bought these goods at an enormous rate. As a result, the United States experienced a gigantic boom in its economy.

The automobile industry was a new industry that was important to this boom. By 1923 the United States was making more than 3 million cars a year. Leading the industry was Henry Ford, who had perfected his system of mass production using the assembly line. The assembly line cut the amount of time it took to produce a car because the cars were assembled by a line of workers rather than one at a time. The assembly line also cuts costs, making cars more affordable. In 1925 a person could buy a new car for about $260.

Another important new industry was air transportation, or aviation. In 1903 Orville and Wilbur Wright made the first flight at Kitty Hawk, North Carolina. After their triumph, the airplane was improved. Then in 1927 Charles Lindbergh, an American airmail pilot, took his plane named the *Spirit of St. Louis* across the Atlantic Ocean. He became a hero all over the world. His flight made people more interested in air travel. Between 1926 and 1930, air travel became a huge commercial industry, or one that is run to make a profit.

Entertainment also helped America's economy to boom. The first commercial radio stations started broadcasting during the 1920s. People listened to the radio to follow sports, hear music, and get important information. More than 800 stations were reaching 10 million families by 1929, making the radio a household appliance. The motion picture business, or movie business, also started in the 1920s. At first only silent films were made, but by 1927 many movies were made with sound. People started going to movies more often, adding to America's economic boom in the 1920s.

(continued)

LA.A.2.2.1(5.1) extends previously learned knowledge and skills of the fourth grade level with increasingly complex reading texts and assignments and tasks (for example, explicit and implicit ideas).
LA.E.2.2.4(5.2) identifies the major information in a nonfiction text.

© Harcourt

Name _____   Date _____

Directions **Complete the graphic organizer.**

Focus Skill # Cause and Effect

Cause

Effect

→

LA.A.2.2.1(5.1) extends previously learned knowledge and skills of the fourth grade level with increasingly complex reading texts and assignments and tasks (for example, explicit and implicit ideas).
LA.E.2.2.1(5.1) understands cause-and-effect relationships in literary texts.

Lesson 2: The Great Depression and the New Deal

Building Vocabulary

Directions Use the vocabulary terms in the box below to complete the sentences.

stock market	bureaucracy	minimum wage
depression	unemployment	hydroelectric dams

1 The factory workers cheered when they learned about the new law that raised the

_____ by $3 per hour.

2 During the _____, the children's parents lost their jobs, so the family moved to a new city.

3 The government lowered _____ by creating programs that gave people jobs.

4 When the _____ crashed on October 29, 1929, the Roaring Twenties ended and a time of little economic growth began.

5 Under the New Deal, the federal government became larger and government

workers formed a _____.

6 In the 1930s the federal government began building _____, or dams that use the water they store to produce electricity.

LA.A.1.2.3(5.1) uses a variety of strategies to determine meaning and increase vocabulary (for example, homonyms, homophones, prefixes, suffixes, word-origins, multiple meanings, antonyms, synonyms, word relationships).

Lesson 3: *Children of the Dust Bowl*

Building Fluency

Directions Part A. Practice reading the terms aloud.

Vocabulary	
New Deal	gales
squatter camps	"dust pneumonia"
northers	windbreaks
roil	

Directions Part B. First, practice reading aloud the phrases. Then, practice reading aloud the sentences.

1 Some of the people / who left Oklahoma and went / to California / had to live in squatter camps.

2 The people of the Panhandle flatlands of Oklahoma / could see the northers coming / from 20 to 30 miles away.

3 The residents of Oklahoma / took shelter when they saw the clouds roil.

4 The strong gales / could bury animals / underneath the dust.

5 Many people caught "dust pneumonia," / a fatal disease that / caused severe damage / to the lungs.

6 One program of the New Deal was / to make windbreaks / from trees / to preserve the land.

Directions Part C. Turn to page 580 in your Student Edition. Read aloud the first paragraph three times. Try to improve your reading each time. Record your best time on the lines below.

Number of words	93
My best time	____
Words per minute	____

LA.A.1.2.4(5.1) uses a variety of strategies to monitor reading in fifth-grade or higher level texts (for example, adjusting reading rate according to purpose and text difficulty, rereading, self-correcting, summarizing, checking other sources, class and group discussions, trying an alternate word).

© Harcourt

Lesson 4: World War II

Reading Primary Sources

Directions After the attack by the Japanese on Pearl Harbor, many Japanese Americans living on the west coast of the United States were sent to live in relocation camps. Clara Breed was the children's librarian at the San Diego Public Library during that time. Before the Japanese families were sent away, Miss Breed gave the children stamped and addressed postcards and asked them to write to her describing what their life was like. She corresponded with them for the length of their stay. The letters and postcards she received are now in the Japanese American National Museum. Below is part of one of the letters Miss Breed received from a Japanese teenager. After you have read the letter, use it to answer the questions on page 165.

April 13, 1942

Dear Miss Breed,

I am in good health and my arm is getting along fine. I received doctor's order so I am allowed to have milk with my meals. The food here is about the same as the food at the county hospital with the exception of less meat here. Now that we have a number of San Diego men working in the kitchens the food has improved quite a bit, especially with the salads. I have heard that we are to receive meat soon, but I think it will be mostly stew because we are not allowed knives, just a spoon and fork as eating utensils. . . .

Sincerely,

Ted

(continued)

LA.E.1.2.1(5.3) reads a variety of literary and informational texts (for example, fiction, drama, poetry, myths, fantasies, historical fiction, biographies, autobiographies, textbooks, manuals, magazines).
LA.E.2.2.4(5.2) identifies the major information in a nonfiction text.

Name _____ Date _____

Directions Use the letter from page 164 to answer the questions that follow.

1 Where is the writer of the letter, and why is he there?

_____

_____

2 Why is the writer sending Miss Breed a letter?

_____

_____

3 Why is the writer of the letter allowed to have milk?

_____

_____

4 Why do you think the people at the relocation camp are not allowed to use knives?

_____

_____

5 What do you think was the reason that many Japanese Americans living on the west coast were sent to relocation camps?

_____

_____

_____

LA.E.1.2.1(5.3) reads a variety of literary and informational texts (for example, fiction, drama, poetry, myths, fantasies, historical fiction, biographies, autobiographies, textbooks, manuals, magazines).
LA.E.2.2.4(5.2) identifies the major information in a nonfiction text.

Name _____   Date _____

Lesson 5: The Allies Win the War

Reading Biographies

Directions Read the passage about Jacqueline Cochran. Then use what you have learned to answer the questions on the next page.

Jacqueline Cochran
Character Trait: Patriotism

Jacqueline Cochran was born in Pensacola, Florida, in 1910. She lived with foster parents. When she was 14 years old, she got a job in a beauty salon. She became a talented beautician and worked in New York City and Miami. Later Cochran started her own successful cosmetics company.

In 1932 Jacqueline Cochran learned to fly an airplane. In 1934 she began competing in flying races and eventually set flying records.

Then, in 1942, Army general Henry Arnold asked Cochran to train civilian women pilots in case there was a shortage of military pilots during World War II. A year later she was named director of the Women's Air Force Service Pilots (WASPs) and helped train more than 1,000 women. Cochran was the first woman to fly a bomber across the Atlantic Ocean during the war. For her patriotism during wartime, Cochran received the Distinguished Service Medal.

After the war, Cochran continued flying. In 1953 she broke the sound barrier. Later she set nine international speed, distance, and altitude jet records. In fact, she held more of these records than any other male or female pilot in history. For all her contributions to the field of aviation, Jacqueline Cochran was inducted into the National Aviation Hall of Fame in 1971. She died in 1980.

(continued)

LA.E.1.2.1(5.3) reads a variety of literary and informational texts (for example, fiction, drama, poetry, myths, fantasies, historical fiction, biographies, autobiographies, textbooks, manuals, magazines).
LA.E.2.2.4(5.2) identifies the major information in a nonfiction text.

Name _____ Date _____

Directions Use what you have learned from the biography on page 166 to answer the questions that follow.

CHARACTER EDUCATION

How did Jacqueline Cochran show her **patriotism** during World War II?

_____

_____

_____

1 How did Cochran become successful in life?

_____

_____

_____

2 What were some honors Cochran received?

_____

_____

3 How did Cochran's achievements affect the lives of other people in the 1930s, 1940s, and 1950s?

_____

_____

_____

© Harcourt

LA.E.1.2.1(5.3) reads a variety of literary and informational texts (for example, fiction, drama, poetry, myths, fantasies, historical fiction, biographies, autobiographies, textbooks, manuals, magazines).
LA.E.1.2.2(5.3) makes inferences and draws conclusions regarding story elements of a fifth grade or higher level text (for example, the traits, actions, and motives of characters; plot development; setting).
LA.E.2.2.4(5.2) identifies the major information in a nonfiction text.

FCAT Test Prep

Directions Read the passage "Florida and World War II" before answering Numbers 1 through 7.

Florida and World War II

The United States entered World War II on December 8, 1941, the day after the Japanese attacked Pearl Harbor. Florida's location, climate, and large areas of flat land made it a perfect place for military bases where soldiers could be trained. It was also the ideal place for training aircraft pilots. Camp Blanding, Jacksonville Naval Air Station, Drew and MacDill Air Fields in Tampa, and the Pensacola Naval Air Base were important bases.

More than 250,000 Floridians served in the United States armed forces in World War II, and about 3,000 of them lost their lives. Because so many men were away, women took jobs in shipyards, in welding shops, and on military bases. They worked on farms, and they volunteered wherever they were needed. Women organized metal drives and money drives, and they planted gardens, called "victory gardens." Many foods were rationed, such as sugar,

coffee, meat, and butter. People learned to do without many items that they were used to having.

While no land battles were fought in the United States during World War II, the war did reach Florida's coast. In 1942 German submarines, called U-boats, sank more than 24 ships off Florida's Atlantic and Gulf coasts. Secret agents from Germany even came onto Florida's shore near Jacksonville at Ponte Vedra Beach. They wanted to blow up railroads and destroy war supplies. They were captured, so no harm was done. After that, the Civil Air Patrol was organized to protect Florida's coast. Volunteers known as spotters kept track of any activity that occurred in the air above Florida's shores.

In 1945 the war ended with the Allies (United States, Britain, France, and Russia) defeating the Axis Powers (Germany, Japan, and Italy). Soldiers returning to Florida found that their state had changed. While agriculture was still important to the state, the war had brought new industries to Florida. Its economy was now more diverse because electronics, plastics, international banking, and tourism had become important.

U.S. Naval Air Station, Florida

Go On ▶

© Harcourt

Directions Now answer Numbers 1 through 7. Base your answers on the passage "Florida and World War II."

1 The Japanese attacked Pearl Harbor on
- Ⓐ December 7, 1941.
- Ⓑ December 8, 1941.
- Ⓒ February 11, 1942.
- Ⓓ May 5, 1945.

2 Florida was a perfect place for military bases because
- Ⓕ many bases were already there.
- Ⓖ it was near the Atlantic Ocean.
- Ⓗ of its location, climate, and flat land.
- Ⓘ Florida sent 250,000 soldiers to war.

3 Women had job opportunities during World War II because
- Ⓐ they were the best workers.
- Ⓑ they volunteered to hold money drives and metal drives.
- Ⓒ so many men were fighting in the war.
- Ⓓ men were used as spotters.

4 Why did secret agents from Germany come to Florida?
- Ⓕ to destroy ships off the coast of Florida
- Ⓖ to get food supplies for German soldiers
- Ⓗ to help Florida's economy
- Ⓘ to blow up railroads and destroy war supplies

5 The Civil Air Patrol was created to
- Ⓐ train soldiers.
- Ⓑ protect Florida's coast.
- Ⓒ improve tourism.
- Ⓓ stop German U-boats from attacking Florida.

6 After World War II, all the following industries were new to Florida EXCEPT
- Ⓕ international banking.
- Ⓖ plastics.
- Ⓗ agriculture.
- Ⓘ electronics.

© Harcourt

Go On ▶

Name _____   Date _____

7 What effects did World War II have on Florida?

READ
THINK
EXPLAIN

_____

_____

_____

_____

_____

_____

_____

_____

_____

_____

_____

_____

_____

_____

_____

_____

_____

_____

_____

_____

_____

Name _____ Date _____

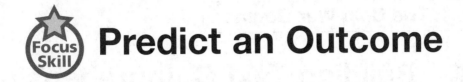

Predict an Outcome

Directions Read the passage below. Then use it to complete the graphic organizer about world leaders and economic growth.

World leadership changed after the end of the Cold War. Today world leadership is based partly on economic strength. It is, therefore, important for nations to trade with one another to maintain strong economies. One possible model for economic leadership is the European Union, or EU.

A group of European leaders met in 1993 to begin the European Union. Member nations of the EU agreed that people, goods, and services could travel freely among their nations. This decision meant lower prices for European consumers. The world leaders who joined the European Union found ways to work together to strengthen each nation's economy. Other national leaders decided to become part of the European Union. In 2004 ten new countries joined the EU on the same day—the most that had ever joined at once. Some of these new member nations had once been part of the Soviet Union.

REMEMBER:
• **When you make predictions, you use information and past experiences to try to determine what will happen next.**

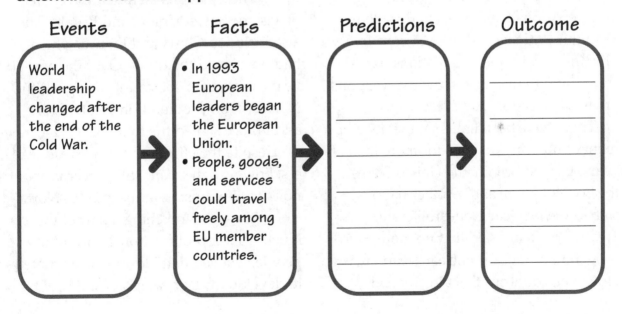

Events	Facts	Predictions	Outcome
World leadership changed after the end of the Cold War.	• In 1993 European leaders began the European Union. • People, goods, and services could travel freely among EU member countries.		

LA.A.2.2.1(5.1) extends previously learned knowledge and skills of the fourth grade level with increasingly complex reading texts and assignments and tasks (for example, explicit and implicit ideas).
LA.E.2.2.4(5.2) identifies the major information in a nonfiction text.

© Harcourt

Name _____ Date _____

Building Text Comprehension
Predict an Outcome

Directions Read the passage below. Use the information you have read to complete the graphic organizer on the next page. Make predictions about the benefits of arms control.

During the Cold War the United States and the Soviet Union took part in an arms race. Each nation tried to build better, stronger weapons than the other. The arms race did not go on forever, though. The world today is different than the world during the Cold War.

The Soviet Union dissolved in 1991. Although Russia is still a superpower, it has an elected president and a constitution. The United States and Russia are working together to prevent another arms race. In 2002 United States President George W. Bush and Russian President Vladimir Putin signed the Moscow Treaty. This treaty said that both nations would shut down thousands of nuclear weapons, or atomic weapons, by 2012.

There have been limits on the development of nuclear weapons for more than 30 years. In 1968 Britain, the United States, the Soviet Union, and 59 other nations signed the Nuclear Non-proliferation Treaty. The treaty said that no more countries should develop nuclear weapons. However, countries that already had

nuclear weapons were allowed to keep them. These nations included the United States, the Soviet Union, and Britain. They also included China and France, which had not signed the treaty. Over the next 30 years, more than 180 countries signed the Nuclear Non-proliferation Treaty. China and France signed the treaty in 1992.

Despite the efforts of many world leaders, however, there are still concerns about nuclear weapons. In January 2003, North Korea chose to stop being a part of the Nuclear Non-proliferation Treaty. Many people believed that North Korea wanted to develop nuclear weapons of its own.

(continued)

LA.A.2.2.1(5.1) extends previously learned knowledge and skills of the fourth grade level with increasingly complex reading texts and assignments and tasks (for example, explicit and implicit ideas).
LA.E.2.2.4(5.2) identifies the major information in a nonfiction text.

© Harcourt

Name _____ Date _____

Predict an Outcome

Focus Skill

Events → **Facts** → **Predictions** → **Outcome**

LA.A.2.2.1(5.1) extends previously learned knowledge and skills of the fourth grade level with increasingly complex reading texts and assignments and tasks (for example, explicit and implicit ideas).

LA.A.2.2.5(5.1) reads and organizes information from multiple sources for a variety of purposes (for example, supporting opinions, predictions, and conclusions; writing a research report; conducting interviews; taking a test; performing tasks).

Lesson 2: *One Giant Leap*

Building Fluency

Directions Part A. Practice reading the terms aloud.

Vocabulary		
satellite	journalists	alien
astronaut	altitudes	solar system
lunar	cockpit	space shuttle

Directions Part B. First, practice reading aloud the phrases. Then, practice reading aloud the sentences.

1. Astronauts must wear / special space equipment and clothing / because they travel / to high altitudes.

2. The control panel, / or place that controls the movements / of the space shuttle, / is located in the cockpit.

3. Before people traveled / to the moon, / the Soviet Union launched a satellite / into space.

4. The first astronaut / to orbit the Earth / was American.

5. The Earth is located / in the solar system.

6. The moon is an alien world / that has remained the same / for millions of years.

7. Astronauts were afraid / of lunar dust / and of sinking into the lunar soil / when they prepared for their trip / to the moon.

Directions Part C. Turn to page 616 in your student edition. Read aloud the first 2 paragraphs three times. Try to improve your reading each time. Record your best time on the lines below.

Number of words	106
My best time	_____
Words per minute	_____

LA.A.1.2.4(5.1) uses a variety of strategies to monitor reading in fifth-grade or higher level texts (for example, adjusting reading rate according to purpose and text difficulty, rereading, self-correcting, summarizing, checking other sources, class and group discussions, trying an alternate word).

© Harcourt

Lesson 3: The Struggle for Equal Rights

Reading Biographies

Directions Read the passage about Mel Martinez. Then use the information to answer the questions below.

Mel Martinez
Character Trait: Citizenship

Mel Martinez was born in Sagua la Grande, Cuba, in 1947. In 1962, at age 15, Martinez came to the United States. He lived with foster parents in Orlando until his family was also able to leave Cuba.

Mel Martinez attended Florida State University and graduated with a degree in law in 1973. He set up a law practice in Orlando. Martinez played an active role in his community and often did volunteer work. In 1984 he was named chair of the Orlando Housing Authority. Then in 1998 he was elected chair of Orange County, Florida.

On January 24, 2001, President George W. Bush selected Martinez to become the nation's twelfth secretary of Housing and Urban Development. He was the first

Cuban American Cabinet member in United States history. During his time in this office, Martinez helped minority and low-income families afford homes. He believed that people of all backgrounds have the right to own property. He also improved the quality and availability of public housing. In November, 2004, Martinez was elected to represent Florida in the United States Senate.

1 What did Martinez accomplish as secretary of Housing and Urban Development?

_____

_____

2 How do you think Mel Martinez has shown his **citizenship**? _____

_____

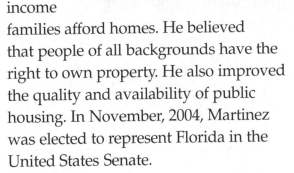

LA.E.1.2.1(5.3) reads a variety of literary and informational texts (for example, fiction, drama, poetry, myths, fantasies, historical fiction, biographies, autobiographies, textbooks, manuals, magazines).
LA.E.1.2.2(5.3) makes inferences and draws conclusions regarding story elements of a fifth grade or higher level text (for example, the traits, actions, and motives of characters; plot development; setting).

Lesson 4: Vietnam War and Protests at Home

Reading Primary Sources

Directions The passage below is from a speech made by President George W. Bush on Veterans Day, 2003. After you have read the passage, use it and what you already know to answer the questions that follow.

DAILY ☼ NEWS

Throughout our history, loyal citizens from every corner of America have willingly assumed the duty of military life. And time after time, in conflicts across the globe, they have proven that democracy is mightier than tyranny. From World War I and World War II, to the conflicts in Korea, Vietnam, and the Persian Gulf . . . our military has built a great tradition of courageous and faithful service. Our veterans have helped bring freedom to countries around the world. Free nations and peoples liberated by American troops are grateful for the long, distinguished line of American veterans who have come to their aid. . . . Now, therefore, I, George W. Bush, President of the United States of America . . . do urge all Americans to observe November 9 through November 15, 2003, as National Veterans Awareness Week. I encourage all Americans to recognize the valor and sacrifice of our veterans through appropriate ceremonies. . . .

1 What do you think President Bush means when he says that "democracy is mightier than tyranny"? _____

_____

2 In what way does President Bush honor the service that members of the military have given to their country? _____

_____

© Harcourt

LA.E.1.2.1(5.3) reads a variety of literary and informational texts (for example, fiction, drama, poetry, myths, fantasies, historical fiction, biographies, autobiographies, textbooks, manuals, magazines).
LA.E.2.2.4(5.2) identifies the major information in a nonfiction text.

Lesson 5: The Cold War Ends

Building Vocabulary

Directions For each sentence, use the context provided to write a definition of the underlined word.

1 The United States and Soviet Union used <u>arms control</u> to limit the number of weapons that each nation may have.

_____

_____

2 When Soviet leader Leonid Brezhnev and President Nixon decided to work together and reduce their number of weapons, there was a period of <u>détente</u>.

_____

_____

3 When planes were hijacked on September 11, 2001, the day went down in history for its horrific acts of <u>terrorism</u>.

_____

_____

4 In times of war, countries hold <u>hostages</u> as prisoners until their demands are met.

_____

_____

5 The United States' budget <u>deficit</u>, or shortage of money, has caused it to lose its rank as economic superpower.

_____

_____

LA.A.2.2.5(5.1) reads and organizes information from multiple sources for a variety of purposes (for example, supporting opinions, predictions, and conclusions; writing a research report; conducting interviews; taking a test; performing tasks).

FCAT Test Prep

Directions Read the passage "Famous Floridians" before answering Numbers 1 through 8.

Famous Floridians

Fernando Bujones, Xavier Cortada, Arturo Sandoval, and Cristina Saralegui are famous Hispanic Floridians. Each of them is involved in the arts or journalism.

Fernando Bujones has been the artistic director for the Orlando Ballet since 2000. Born in Miami, Florida, Bujones has been dancing for more than 30 years. He has performed in 34 countries with about 60 dance companies. As artistic director, Bujones has improved the Orlando Ballet company and has expanded the number of ballets it performs. In 2002 he was inducted into the Florida Artists Hall of Fame, Florida's highest cultural honor.

Xavier Cortada is an artist who uses the Internet in group art projects. Born in Cuba, he now lives in Miami. He has worked with groups throughout the world to create community murals. He often speaks on the use of art to help bring about social change. In his work he has explored topics such as racism, violence, and poverty. Winner of the Millennium International Volunteer Award, he has created art for the White House and the Miami Art Museum.

Arturo Sandoval is a world-famous trumpet player. Born in Artemisa, Cuba, Sandoval began his trumpet studies at age 12. Today he is respected as both a jazz trumpet player and a classical artist. A resident of Florida, he has been a guest artist with symphony orchestras throughout the world. He has won numerous Grammy awards and has published music books with recordings for young trumpet students. In 2004 he was a professor and an artist in residence at Florida International University.

Recognized as a role model for Hispanic women, Cristina Saralegui is a journalist and a television and radio personality. Born in Havana, Cuba, she came from a family with a background in publishing. In 1960 she left Cuba and arrived in Miami. After getting a college degree in communications and creative writing, Saralegui worked for several Latin American magazines. In 1989 she became the host of *The Cristina Show*, which has won ten Emmy awards and is seen in Latin America and in most European countries. In 2001 Saralegui received a leadership award from the Hispanic Heritage Awards Foundation.

Cristina Saralegui

© Harcourt

Go On ▶

Directions Now answer Numbers 1 through 8. Base your answers on the passage "Famous Floridians."

1 Since he became artistic director for the Orlando Ballet, Fernando Bujones has

Ⓐ performed with about 60 dance companies.

Ⓑ written a book about ballet for young ballet students.

Ⓒ traveled to Miami with the dance company.

Ⓓ expanded the number of ballets the company performs.

2 What does Xavier Cortada use in group art projects?

Ⓕ television

Ⓖ the Internet

Ⓗ mosaics

Ⓘ watercolors

3 In his art work, Cortada explores all of the following topics EXCEPT

Ⓐ education.

Ⓑ racism.

Ⓒ poverty.

Ⓓ violence.

4 What do all the people discussed in the passage have in common?

Ⓕ They are all journalists.

Ⓖ They are all men.

Ⓗ They are all Hispanic.

Ⓘ They are all artists.

5 Who is an artist in residence at Florida International University?

Ⓐ Cristina Saralegui

Ⓑ Arturo Sandoval

Ⓒ Xavier Cortada

Ⓓ Fernando Bujones

6 Cristina Saralegui is the host of a show that is seen

Ⓕ only in the United States.

Ⓖ in Australia and Asia.

Ⓗ in Latin America and in most European countries.

Ⓘ in the Miami Art Museum.

Go On ▶

Name _____ Date _____

7 Why do you think Cristina Saralegui is a role model for Hispanic women?

READ
THINK
EXPLAIN

_____

_____

_____

_____

_____

_____

_____

8 Fernando Bujones, Xavier Cortada, Arturo Sandoval, and Cristina Saralegui are all Floridians. List ways they are all alike and ways they are different.

READ
THINK
EXPLAIN

_____

_____

_____

_____

_____

_____

_____

_____

STOP

© Harcourt

Name _____ Date _____

 # Compare and Contrast

Directions Read the passage below. Then use it to complete the graphic organizer about the history of Mexico and Florida.

During the 1500s the Spanish claimed Mexico. Mexico was under Spanish rule for about 300 years. Then, after a revolution, Mexico won its independence from Spain. Eventually, Mexico became an independent country.

During the 1500s the Spanish also claimed Florida. Florida was under Spanish rule until 1763, when Spain gave Florida to the British. However, in 1783, after the Revolutionary War, Florida was once again under Spanish rule. Spain ruled Florida until 1819, when a treaty gave Florida to the United States. Eventually, Florida became the twenty-seventh state of the United States.

REMEMBER:

• To compare two things is to find out how they are alike.

• To contrast two things is to find out how they are different.

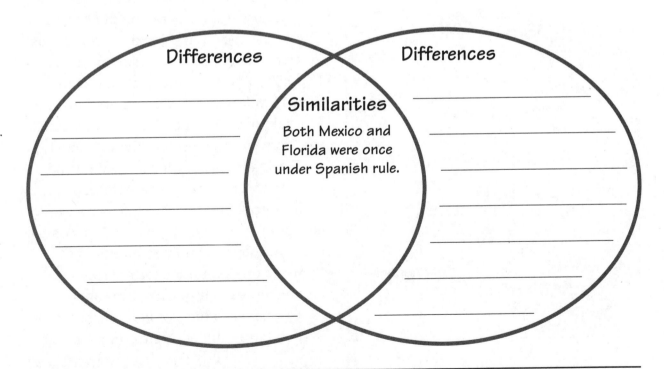

LA.A.2.2.1(5.1) extends previously learned knowledge and skills of the fourth grade level with increasingly complex reading texts and assignments and tasks (for example, explicit and implicit ideas).
LA.A.2.2.7(5.1) extends the expectations of the fourth grade with increasingly complex reading selections, assignments and tasks (for example, textual organization, comparison and contrast).
LA.E.2.2.4(5.2) identifies the major information in a nonfiction text.

© Harcourt

Name _____ Date _____

Building Text Comprehension
Compare and Contrast

Directions Read the passage below about the Mexican state of Chiapas and Florida. As you read, compare and contrast the two states. Then complete the graphic organizer on the next page.

Chiapas is one of Mexico's 31 states. It is located in the southern part of the country. Its southwestern border is the Pacific Ocean. Chiapas has an area of about 28,528 square miles (73,888 sq km) and a population of more than 3 million. Its natural regions are the Pacific Coastal Plain, the Sierra Madre de Chiapas, the Central Depression, the Central Highland Plateau, the Northern Mountains, the Eastern Mountains, and the Gulf Coastal Plain.

Chiapas has many rivers and hills as well as volcanoes. In addition, Chiapas has hundreds of lakes and many waterfalls. The climate of Chiapas is tropical, with a lot of rain in the summer. Some products of Chiapas are petroleum and woods used to make furniture and carvings.

Florida is one of 50 states in the United States. It is located in the southern part of the country. It is bordered by the Atlantic Ocean and the Gulf of Mexico. Florida has an area of about 58,556 square miles (151,659 sq km) and a population of more than 15 million. Its natural regions are the Coastal Lowlands, the Marianna Lowlands, the highland regions, and the wetlands.

Florida has a very long coastline and more than 7,800 lakes. The state also has many rivers. Because the state has a low elevation, it is generally warm. Most days are sunny, but on summer afternoons there are often thunderstorms. The state also experiences tropical storms and hurricanes. Some products of Florida are strawberries, citrus, lumber, petroleum, and fish.

(continued)

Chiapas (map)

CAMPECHE
VERACRUZ   TABASCO
Palenque Ruinas
Pichucalco   Tila
Simojovel
Larrainzair   Ococingo
Teneiapa
Tuxtla Gutierrez   San C. de Las Casas   Altamirano
CHIAPAS
Sierra Norte de Chiapas
Comitan   Las Margaritas
Arriaga   La Angostura Dam
Tonala   Sierra Madre de Chiapas
Ciudad Cuauhtemoc
GUATEMALA
Huixtla
PACIFIC OCEAN   Tapachula
OAXACA

© Harcourt

LA.A.2.2.1(5.1) extends previously learned knowledge and skills of the fourth grade level with increasingly complex reading texts and assignments and tasks (for example, explicit and implicit ideas).
LA.A.2.2.7(5.1) extends the expectations of the fourth grade with increasingly complex reading selections, assignments and tasks (for example, textual organization, comparison and contrast).
LA.E.2.2.4(5.2) identifies the major information in a nonfiction text.

Name _____ Date _____

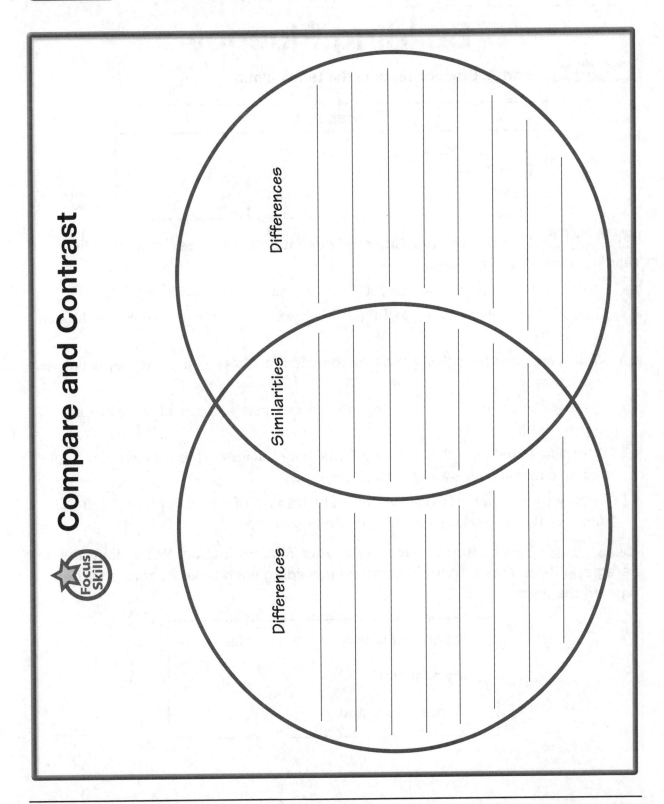

★ Focus Skill

Compare and Contrast

Differences

Similarities

Differences

LA.A.2.2.1(5.1) extends previously learned knowledge and skills of the fourth grade level with increasingly complex reading texts and assignments and tasks (for example, explicit and implicit ideas).
LA.A.2.2.7(5.1) extends the expectations of the fourth grade with increasingly complex reading selections, assignments and tasks (for example, textual organization, comparison and contrast).

Lesson 2: *Save My Rainforest*

Building Fluency

Directions Part A. Practice reading the terms aloud.

Vocabulary	
Selva Lacandona	envy
Tuxtla Gutiérrez	*tortilla*
mango	*abuela*

Directions Part B. First, practice reading aloud the phrases. Then, practice reading aloud the sentences.

1 Selva Lacandona is more than an 800-mile / walk from Mexico City.

2 Omar and his father travel / to Tuxtla Gutiérrez / to see the governor / of the state of Chiapas.

3 While Omar and his father / travel to the rain forest, / they see banana plantations and *mango* trees.

4 Omar watches / with envy / as the other boys / play soccer, / because he longs / to play.

5 When Omar and his father / walk into the poor villages, / the villagers come out / and give them oranges and *tortilla* chips.

6 Omar worries / about his *abuela* / when he learns / of the earthquake / that damages the hospital / where his grandmother is.

Directions Part C. Turn to page 647 in your Student Edition. Read aloud the first paragraph three times. Try to improve your reading each time. Record your best time on the lines below.

Number of words	69
My best time	_____
Words per minute	_____

© Harcourt

LA.A.1.2.4(5.1) uses a variety of strategies to monitor reading in fifth-grade or higher level texts (for example, adjusting reading rate according to purpose and text difficulty, rereading, self-correcting, summarizing, checking other sources, class and group discussions, trying an alternate word).

Name _____ Date _____

Reading Maps and Globes

Directions Use the map below to answer the questions that follow.

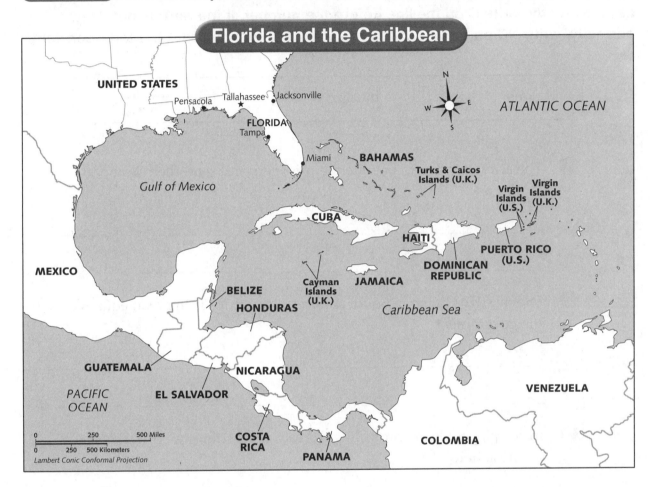

Florida and the Caribbean

1 Which Caribbean country is directly south of Florida? _____

2 In what body of water are Cuba, Jamaica, Haiti, and the Dominican Republic

located? _____

3 In which direction is Jamaica from Florida? _____

4 What bodies of water border Florida? _____

LA.A.2.2.5(5.1) reads and organizes information from multiple sources for a variety of purposes (for example, supporting opinions, predictions, and conclusions; writing a research report; conducting interviews; taking a test; performing tasks).
LA.A.2.2.8(5.1) extends previously learned knowledge and skills of the fourth grade with increasingly complex reading texts and assignments and tasks (for example, using reference materials and processes).

Lesson 4: Challenges in South America

Building Vocabulary

Directions Each vocabulary term is found in a sentence below. If the term is used correctly, write *C* on the line before the number. If the term is not used correctly, write *NC* on the line. Then rewrite the sentence using the term correctly.

liberate	mestizo	deforestation

_____ **1** The army decided to liberate the prisoners and send them home to their families.

_____

_____

_____ **2** The mestizos living in South American countries wanted an equal voice in the government.

_____

_____

_____ **3** In Brazil, people are protecting the rain forests through programs such as deforestation.

_____

_____

© Harcourt

LA.A.1.2.3(5.1) uses a variety of strategies to determine meaning and increase vocabulary (for example, homonyms, homophones, prefixes, suffixes, word-origins, multiple meanings, antonyms, synonyms, word relationships).
LA.A.2.2.1(5.1) extends previously learned knowledge and skills of the fourth grade level with increasingly complex reading texts and assignments and tasks (for example, explicit and implicit ideas).

Name _____ Date _____

Reading Biographies

Directions Read the passage about Roberta Lynn Bondar. Then answer the question below.

Roberta Lynn Bondar
Character Trait: Self-Control

Roberta Lynn Bondar was born on December 4, 1945, in Sault St. Marie, Ontario, Canada. As a child she enjoyed making rocket models and playing space games. She also had a collection of NASA posters and hoped that someday she would represent her country as an astronaut. Bondar graduated from college with degrees in zoology (the study of animals) and biology (the study of living things). Today Bondar is also a medical doctor specializing in neurology, which deals with diseases of the nervous system.

In 1983 Bondar became one of the first Canadian astronauts to be trained at NASA. Then, in 1992, she achieved one of her goals by becoming the first Canadian woman in space.

Bondar was on the space shuttle *Discovery* as a payload specialist. The mission lasted eight days. While in space, Bondar did experiments in life science and materials science in the Spacelab. Bondar described being in space as feeling as if she were hanging by her heels with her head down. After completing her successful space mission, Bondar decided to retire from being an astronaut and spend her time doing research.

Bondar has received many awards for her work as an astronaut, a neurologist, and a researcher. These awards include the Canada 125 Medal, the Order of Canada, the NASA Space Medal, and the 1995 Women's Intercultural Network International Women's Day Award.

1 How did Roberta Lynn Bondar demonstrate **self-control**? _____

_____

LA.E.1.2.1(5.3) reads a variety of literary and informational texts (for example, fiction, drama, poetry, myths, fantasies, historical fiction, biographies, autobiographies, textbooks, manuals, magazines).
LA.E.1.2.2(5.3) makes inferences and draws conclusions regarding story elements of a fifth grade or higher level text (for example, the traits, actions, and motives of characters; plot development; setting).

FCAT Test Prep

Directions Read the passage "NAFTA" before answering Numbers 1 through 8.

NAFTA

Many countries have signed free-trade agreements to increase international trade. A free-trade agreement is a treaty in which countries agree not to charge tariffs, or taxes, on goods they buy from and sell to each other. The United States, Mexico, and Canada have a free-trade agreement. The North American Free Trade Agreement (NAFTA) was signed in November 1993.

NAFTA has helped make North America the world's largest free-trade area, with a total gross domestic product (total value of the goods and services produced in the three countries) of approximately $11.4 trillion. NAFTA's

United States

Canada

Mexico

purpose was to open up markets to make the selling of goods and services easier among the three countries. Another of its goals was to create new opportunities for employment, to improve environmental laws, and to give consumers more choices.

NAFTA has provided many benefits for the three North American countries. Each country has increased its exports to the other two countries. Because of NAFTA, investors from one NAFTA country have been willing to invest in markets in the other two countries. Investments from countries outside of NAFTA have also increased. This increase in investment has had a positive effect on the economies of the United States, Canada, and Mexico.

Consumers, the users of the products and services, also benefit from NAFTA. Consumers often pay less for products and have more choices. This leads to a higher standard of living for people in each country.

NAFTA is committed to protecting the environment. Environmental laws are enforced in all three countries. Also, NAFTA partners regularly share ways to conserve and protect resources. Many people agree that NAFTA has benefited farmers, workers, manufacturers, and consumers in the United States, Canada, and Mexico.

© Harcourt

Go On ▶

FCAT

Directions Now answer Numbers 1 through 8. Base your answers on the passage "NAFTA."

1 A treaty in which countries agree not to charge tariffs, or taxes, on goods they buy from and sell to each other is
- Ⓐ a free-trade agreement.
- Ⓑ e-commerce.
- Ⓒ a free enterprise economy.
- Ⓓ an embargo on exports.

2 What is NAFTA?
- Ⓕ the North American Finance and Trade Alliance
- Ⓖ the North American Fair Treaty Act
- Ⓗ the North American Federal Trade Act
- Ⓘ the North American Free Trade Agreement

3 The purpose of NAFTA is to
- Ⓐ increase trade to European countries.
- Ⓑ increase trade among the United States, Canada, and Mexico.
- Ⓒ protect consumers.
- Ⓓ establish international guidelines for exporting goods.

4 Which of the following statements is CORRECT?
- Ⓕ NAFTA has made North America the world's largest free-trade area.
- Ⓖ NAFTA has decreased trade in North America.
- Ⓗ NAFTA is an agreement between the United States and Cuba.
- Ⓘ NAFTA has decreased Mexico's gross domestic product.

5 Under NAFTA consumers often
- Ⓐ pay less for products and have fewer choices.
- Ⓑ pay more for products and have fewer choices.
- Ⓒ pay less for products and have more choices.
- Ⓓ pay more for products and have more choices.

6 NAFTA has encouraged all of the following EXCEPT
- Ⓕ strengthening of environmental regulations.
- Ⓖ increasing tariffs on exports.
- Ⓗ fair rules of trade.
- Ⓘ investments from member nations and from foreign countries in United States, Canadian, and Mexican markets.

© Harcourt

Go On ▶

7 One of NAFTA's purposes is to strengthen environmental regulations. Why might protecting the environment be important to NAFTA countries?

READ
THINK
EXPLAIN

_____

_____

_____

_____

_____

_____

_____

_____

8 What effect has NAFTA had on trade among the United States, Canada, and Mexico?

READ
THINK
EXPLAIN

_____

_____

_____

_____

_____

_____

_____

_____

STOP

© Harcourt